# Extending Tables

A table is an organized way to show a pattern.

| Weeks | Days |
|-------|------|
| 1 | 7 |
| 3 | 21 |
| 5 | 35 |
| 6 | 42 |
| 8 | ? |

Each pair of values follows some rule. If you can find a rule that works for all the pairs, you can extend the table.

What is the missing number in this table?

## Step 1

Find a rule for the pattern.

The first 4 weeks are shown.
You can divide to find the pattern.

$42 \div 6 = 7$
$35 \div 5 = 7$
$21 \div 3 = 7$
$7 \div 1 = 7$

There are 7 days in one week.

## Step 2

Use your rule to find the missing number.

Multiply the days in 1 week by the number of weeks.

$8 \times 7 = 56$

The missing number is 56.

Complete each table.

**1.**

| Cars | Wheels |
|------|--------|
| 1 | 4 |
| 2 | 8 |
| 3 | |
| 4 | 16 |
| 8 | 32 |

**2.**

| Old Price | New Price |
|-----------|-----------|
| $63 | $53 |
| $48 | $38 |
| | $31 |
| $37 | $27 |
| $26 | $16 |

**3.**

| Weight of Salad in Ounces | 6 | 10 | 14 | 18 |
|---------------------------|---|----|----|----|
| Total Weight of Container in Ounces | 9 | 13 | 17 | |

Name _____

# Extending Tables

Find the missing numbers.

1.

| Number of Cats | Number of Legs |
|---|---|
| 1 | 4 |
| 2 | |
| 3 | 12 |
| 4 | 16 |
| | 32 |

2.

| Money Earned | Money Saved |
|---|---|
| $25 | $15 |
| $32 | $22 |
| $43 | |
| | $47 |
| $73 | $63 |

3.

| Touchdowns | Points |
|---|---|
| 1 | 6 |
| 2 | 12 |
| 3 | |
| | 36 |
| 8 | 48 |

For **4** and **5**, use the table at the right.

4. How much money would 9 T-shirts cost?

_____

| T-shirts | Cost |
|---|---|
| 1 | $8 |
| 3 | $24 |
| 5 | $40 |

5. **Strategy Practice** How much more money do 10 T-shirts cost than 6 T-shirts? Explain how you found your answer.

_____

_____

_____

6. **Number Sense** Bob has 3 bookshelves that hold a total of 27 books. He adds a fourth shelf and now has 36 books. If he adds 2 more shelves, how many books can he have in total?

_____

7. What is the missing number in the table below?

| In | 3 | 5 | 8 | 15 |
|---|---|---|---|---|
| Out | 9 | 11 | 14 | |

**A** 21      **B** 25      **C** 30      **D** 45

# Writing Rules for Situations

When working with tables, it is important to find a rule that works for all pairs of numbers. The rule tells how to find one of the numbers in a pair.

| Old Price | New Price |
|-----------|-----------|
| $15 | $10 |
| $22 | $17 |
| $28 | $23 |
| $37 | $32 |
| $51 | $46 |

Each pair of numbers in the table to the left follows a rule. If you can find a rule that works, you can extend the table.

### Step 1

Find the pattern. Check the first pair of numbers to see how the first number changed to become the second number.

$15 - 10 = 5$

A rule for the first pair of numbers is "subtract 5."

### Step 2

See if this rule works for all the values.

$22 - 17 = 5$      $37 - 32 = 5$

$28 - 23 = 5$      $51 - 46 = 5$

The rule "subtract 5" works for every pair of values.

Find the missing numbers in each table.
Write a rule for the table.

**1.**

| Earned | Spent |
|--------|-------|
| $21 | $14 |
| $30 | $23 |
| $42 | |
| $48 | $41 |
| $59 | |

**2.**

| Teams | Players |
|-------|---------|
| 3 | 27 |
| 8 | 72 |
| 6 | |
| 9 | |
| 2 | 18 |

**3.**

| Tickets | Cost |
|---------|------|
| 2 | $1 |
| 6 | $3 |
| 12 | |
| 10 | $5 |
| 20 | |

_____    _____    _____

**4. Number Sense** Joe said that by using the information in Exercise 2 there would be 250 players if there were 25 teams. Is that correct? Explain.

_____

_____

Name _____

# Writing Rules for Situations

Find the missing numbers in each table.
Write a rule for the table.

1.

| Max's Age | Carol's Age |
|---|---|
| 7 | 13 |
| 10 | |
| 14 | 20 |
| 18 | 24 |
| | 31 |

2.

| Tricycles | Wheels |
|---|---|
| 5 | 15 |
| 3 | 9 |
| 7 | |
| | 27 |
| 2 | 6 |

3.

| Old Price | New Price |
|---|---|
| $25 | $18 |
| $16 | $9 |
| | $32 |
| $53 | $46 |
| $72 | |

For **4** and **5**, use the table at the right.

4. The table shows the number of players on a volleyball team. What is a rule for the table?

_____

| Players | Teams |
|---|---|
| 24 | 4 |
| 48 | 8 |
| 36 | 6 |
| 30 | 5 |

5. **Explain It** If there are 12 teams, how many players will there be? Explain how you found your answer.

_____

_____

6. How many miles can Nick travel in 5 hours? 6 hours?

| Hours | 1 | 2 | 3 | 4 |
|---|---|---|---|---|
| Miles | 60 | 120 | 180 | 240 |

_____

7. The table shows how many CDs Jim and Ken each own after joining a CD club. Which is a rule that works for this table?

| Jim | 8 | 12 | 20 | 30 |
|---|---|---|---|---|
| Ken | 16 | 20 | 28 | 38 |

**A** Add 8          **C** Subtract 10

**B** Multiply by 2   **D** Divide by 2

Name _____

# Geometric Patterns

Like number patterns, geometric patterns can have figures that grow. To extend geometric patterns follow the same steps as you would for number patterns.

Below is a pattern of squares.

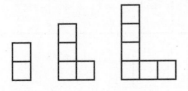

| Number of Figure | 1 | 2 | 3 | 4 | 5 |
|---|---|---|---|---|---|
| Number of Squares | 2 | 4 | 6 | | |

**Step 1**

Look at the pattern. See how the figure has changed.

Each figure grows by 1 square in height and 1 square in width.

Each figure grows by 2 squares.

**Step 2**

Make the next two figures.

**Step 3**

Fill in the table.

| Number of Figure | 1 | 2 | 3 | 4 | 5 |
|---|---|---|---|---|---|
| Number of Squares | 2 | 4 | 6 | 8 | 10 |

Draw the next two towers in the pattern. Use grid paper. Find the missing numbers in each table.

1.

| Number of Stories | 1 | 2 | 3 | 4 | 5 |
|---|---|---|---|---|---|
| Number of Blocks | 4 | 8 | 12 | | |

2.

| Length of Sides | 1 | 2 | 3 | 4 | 5 |
|---|---|---|---|---|---|
| Sum of All Sides | 5 | 10 | 15 | | |

1  2  3

1  2  3

3. **Number Sense** If there were 10 stories in Exercise 1, how many blocks would there be? Explain.

_____

Name _____

# Geometric Patterns

Draw the next two figures in the pattern.
Find the missing numbers in each table.

**1.**

| Number of Stories | 1 | 2 | 3 | 4 | 5 |
|---|---|---|---|---|---|
| Number of Blocks | 5 | 10 | 15 | | |

**2.**

| Number of Stories | 1 | 2 | 3 | 4 | 5 |
|---|---|---|---|---|---|
| Number of Blocks | 2 | 4 | 6 | | |

**3.**

| Length of Each Side | 1 | 2 | 3 | 4 | 5 |
|---|---|---|---|---|---|
| Sum of All Sides | 3 | 6 | 9 | | |

1  2  3

**4.**

| Number of Stories | 1 | 2 | 3 | 4 | 5 |
|---|---|---|---|---|---|
| Number of Blocks | 6 | 12 | 18 | | |

**5. Explain It** Use Exercise 4. How could you find how many blocks there were in 20 stories? How many blocks would there be?

_____

_____

_____

**6.** Which is a rule for the table below?

| In | 3 | 9 | 4 | 7 |
|---|---|---|---|---|
| Out | 7 | 13 | 8 | 11 |

**A** Add 4

**B** Multiply 2

**C** Multiply 4

**D** Add 5

# Problem Solving: Act It Out and Use Reasoning

Izzie has 12 coins. Four of the coins are quarters. He has 2 more dimes than nickels. How many of each coin does he have?

You can use logical reasoning to find the answer. You may be able to determine information that is not told.

| What do I know? | What do I need to find out? | What can I determine from the information? |
|---|---|---|
| Izzie has 12 coins.<br><br>4 of the coins are quarters.<br><br>Izzie has 2 more dimes than nickels. | How many dimes does Izzie have?<br><br>How many nickels does Izzie have? | If 4 of the 12 coins are quarters, Izzie has a total of 8 dimes and nickels. |

You can act it out to find how many dimes and nickels Izzie has.

Take 8 two-color counters. Find combinations so that one color will have 2 more than the other. If you try 4 and 4, the difference is 0, so try 5 and 3. It works.

So, Izzie has 4 quarters, 5 dimes, and 3 nickels.

---

Solve. Find the number of each kind of object in the collection.

1. **Kim's Music Video Collection**

   13 videos in all
   4 concert videos
   3 more rap videos than pop videos

   Concert videos = ☐

   Rap videos = ☐

   Pop videos = ☐

2. **Molly's Art Collection**

   5 paintings
   3 more sculptures than mosaics
   16 pieces in all

   Paintings = ☐

   Sculptures = ☐

   Mosaics = ☐

Name _____

# Problem Solving: Act It Out and Use Reasoning

Solve. Find the number of each kind of object in the collection.

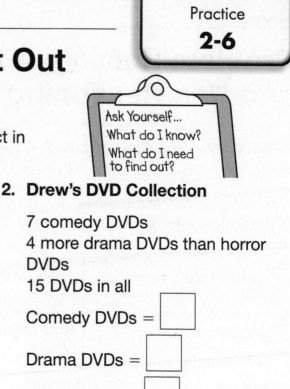

Ask Yourself...
What do I know?
What do I need to find out?

1. **Sue's Card Collection**

   8 packs of baseball cards
   3 fewer packs of hockey cards than football cards
   17 packs in all

   Baseball cards = [ ]

   Hockey cards = [ ]

   Football cards = [ ]

2. **Drew's DVD Collection**

   7 comedy DVDs
   4 more drama DVDs than horror DVDs
   15 DVDs in all

   Comedy DVDs = [ ]

   Drama DVDs = [ ]

   Horror DVDs = [ ]

3. **Strategy Practice** Mike is 8 years older than Kyle. Kyle is 6 years old. The sum of Mike's, Kyle's, and Jamal's ages is 23. How many years old is Jamal?

   _____

4. Miranda has 24 CDs in her collection. Of those CDs, 10 are pop CDs. She has 6 more country CDs than jazz CDs. How many country CDs does Miranda have?

   _____

5. Curt has 12 models in all. Three of the models are airplanes. Curt has 5 more models of cars than boats. How many models of cars does Curt have?

   _____

6. Stevie, Lindsey, and Christine are the lead singers in a band. They will sing 18 songs. Lindsey will sing 8 songs. Christine will sing 6 fewer songs than Stevie. How many songs will Stevie sing?

   **A** 2　　　　**B** 4　　　　**C** 6　　　　**D** 8

Name _____

# Representing Numbers

Use a place-value chart to help you write a number in standard form.

Write four hundred twenty thousand, three hundred fifty-nine in standard form.

**Step 1:** Write 420 in the thousands period.

**Step 2:** Write 359 in the ones period.

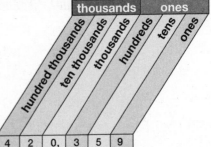

The standard form is 420,359.

Each digit in 420,359 has a different *place value* and *value*. The *place value* of the digit 3 is the hundreds place. This digit has a *value* of 300.

Write each number in standard form.

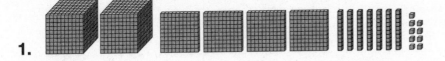

**1.** _____

**2.** 7 ten thousands + 5 thousands + 8 hundreds + _____
1 ten + 0 ones

Write the word form and tell the value of the underlined digit for each number.

**3.** 4,6̲32 _____

_____

**4.** 7̲,129 _____

_____

**5.** 13,57̲2 _____

_____

**6. Number Sense** Write a six-digit number with a 5 in
the ten thousands place and a 2 in the ones place. _____

Name _____

# Representing Numbers

Write each number in standard form.

1.    _____

2.  8 ten thousands + 4 thousands +
    9 hundreds + 4 tens + 7 ones        _____

Write the word form and tell the value of the underlined digit for
each number.

3.  76,239  _____

    _____

4.  823,774  _____

    _____

5.  **Number Sense**  Write the number that has 652 in
    the ones period and 739 in the thousands period.  _____

During a weekend at the Movie Palace Theaters, 24,875 tickets
were sold. Add the following to the number of tickets sold.

6.  100 tickets _____        7.  1,000 tickets _____

8.  Which of the following numbers has a 5 in the
    ten thousands place?

    **A** 652,341      **B** 562,341      **C** 462,541      **D** 265,401

9.  **Writing to Explain**  Explain how you know the 6 in the number 364,021 is
    **NOT** in the thousands place.

    _____

    _____

# Place Value Relationships

In the number 330, what is the relationship between the value of
the digit 3 in each place?

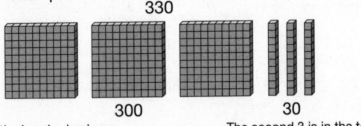

330

300                    30

The first 3 is in the hundreds place.
Its value is 300.

The second 3 is in the tens place.
Its value is 30.

Since 300 is ten times as great as 30, the first 3 is worth 10 times
as much as the second 3. When two digits next to each other in
a number are the same, the one on the left is always 10 times as
great as the one on the right.

Name the values of the given digits in the numbers below.

**1.** the 4s in 440 _____

**2.** the 8s in 8,800 _____

Write the relationship between the values of the given digits.

**3.** the 6s in 660

_____

**4.** the 8s in 8,800

_____

**5. Reason** In the number 550, is the value of the 5 in the tens
place ten times greater than the value of the 5 in the hundreds
place? Explain why or why not.

_____

**6. Reason** Is the relationship between the 6s in 664 and 668
different in any way? Explain why or why not.

_____

# Place Value Relationships

Name the values of the given digits in the numbers below.

1. the 4s in 244 _____

2. the 2s in 2,200 _____

3. the 5s in 6,755 _____

4. the 7s in 770 _____

5. the 6s in 6,600 _____

6. the 9s in 3,994 _____

7. the 8s in 6,588 _____

8. the 3s in 3,312 _____

9. the 1s in 5,114 _____

10. the 2s in 2,226 _____

11. the 7s in 4,777 _____

12. the 9s in 39,990 _____

13. What is the relationship between the 6s in the number 6,647?

_____

_____

_____

_____

_____

14. What is the relationship between the 3s in the number 9,338?

_____

_____

_____

_____

_____

15. **Writing to Explain** In your own words, explain the place-value relationship when the same two digits are next to each other in a multi-digit number.

_____

_____

_____

16. Which of the following names the value of the 5s in the number 1,557?

**A** 50 and 5  **B** 500 and 50  **C** 5,000 and 50  **D** 5,000 and 500

Name _____

# Comparing Numbers

Use these symbols to compare numbers.

**< is less than**        **> is greater than**        **= is equal to**

Compare 1,375 and 1,353.

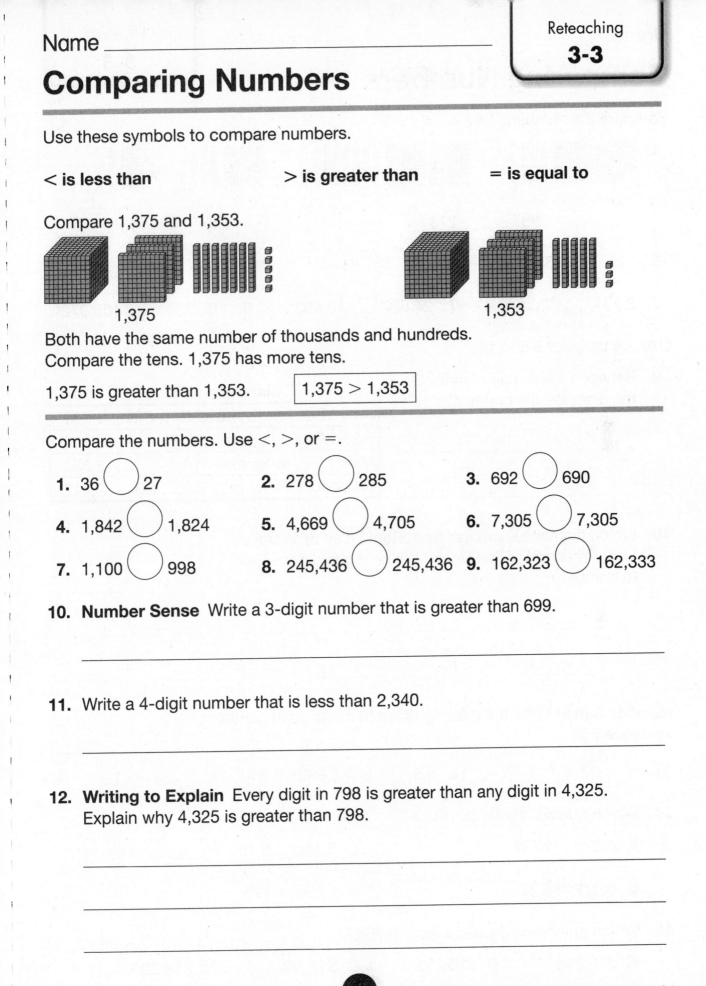

1,375                                        1,353

Both have the same number of thousands and hundreds.
Compare the tens. 1,375 has more tens.

1,375 is greater than 1,353.        | 1,375 > 1,353 |

Compare the numbers. Use <, >, or =.

**1.** 36 ◯ 27

**2.** 278 ◯ 285

**3.** 692 ◯ 690

**4.** 1,842 ◯ 1,824

**5.** 4,669 ◯ 4,705

**6.** 7,305 ◯ 7,305

**7.** 1,100 ◯ 998

**8.** 245,436 ◯ 245,436

**9.** 162,323 ◯ 162,333

**10. Number Sense** Write a 3-digit number that is greater than 699.

_____

**11.** Write a 4-digit number that is less than 2,340.

_____

**12. Writing to Explain** Every digit in 798 is greater than any digit in 4,325.
Explain why 4,325 is greater than 798.

_____

_____

_____

Name _____

# Comparing Numbers

Compare the numbers. Use <, >, or =.

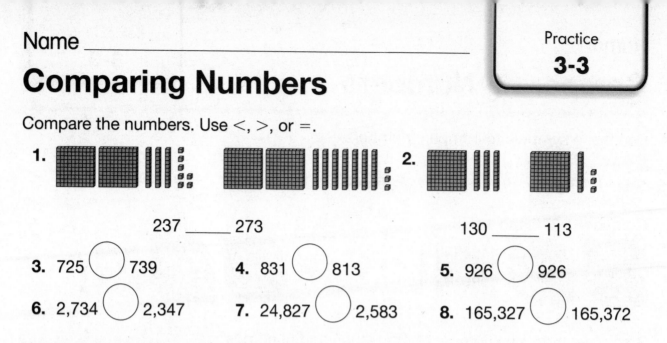

237 _____ 273          130 _____ 113

**3.** 725 ◯ 739     **4.** 831 ◯ 813     **5.** 926 ◯ 926

**6.** 2,734 ◯ 2,347     **7.** 24,827 ◯ 2,583     **8.** 165,327 ◯ 165,372

Use the table for **9** and **10**.

**9.** Between which pair of cities is the distance the greatest?

_____

_____

| Distance in Miles | |
| --- | --- |
| New York, NY, to Rapid City, SD | 1,701 |
| Rapid City, SD, to Miami, FL | 2,167 |
| Miami, FL, to Seattle, WA | 3,334 |
| Portland, OR, to Little Rock, AR | 2,217 |

**10.** Which distance is greater, from Rapid City to Miami or from Portland to Little Rock? Which digits did you use to compare?

_____

_____

**Number Sense** Write the missing digits to make each number sentence true.

**11.** 7 ☐ 7 < 713     **12.** 5,8 ☐ 5 > 5,889     **13.** 43, ☐ 64 = 43,2 ☐ 4

**14.** Which number sentence is true?

   **A** 4,375 > 4,722          **C** 5,106 = 5,160

   **B** 6,372 > 6,327          **D** 7,095 < 795

**15.** Which number is greater than 318,264?

   **A** 318,246     **B** 318,255     **C** 316,842     **D** 318,295

Name _____

# Ordering Numbers

You can use a number line to compare two numbers. Which is greater, 33,430 or 33,515?

**Step 1** Plot the first number on a number line:

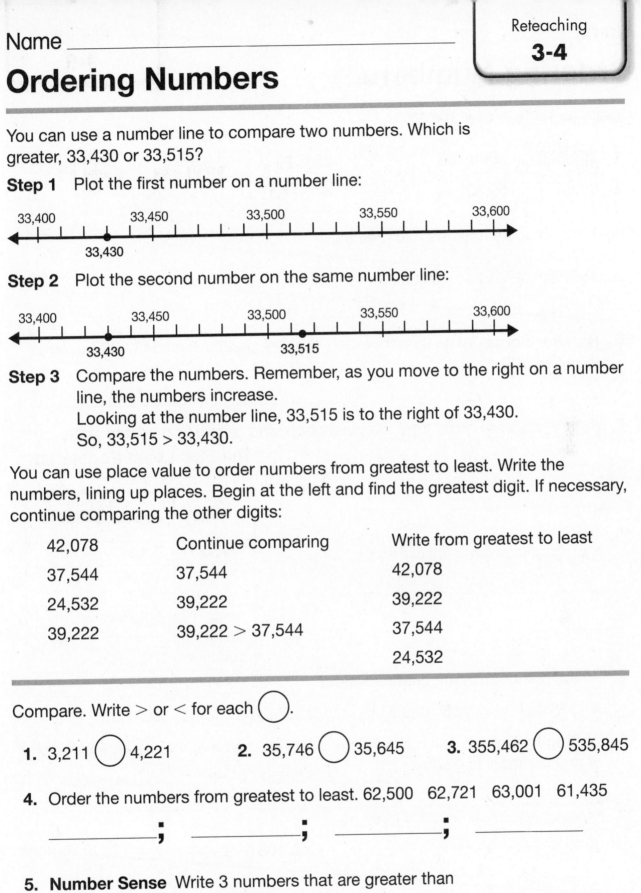

**Step 2** Plot the second number on the same number line:

**Step 3** Compare the numbers. Remember, as you move to the right on a number line, the numbers increase.
Looking at the number line, 33,515 is to the right of 33,430.
So, 33,515 > 33,430.

You can use place value to order numbers from greatest to least. Write the numbers, lining up places. Begin at the left and find the greatest digit. If necessary, continue comparing the other digits:

| | Continue comparing | Write from greatest to least |
|---|---|---|
| 42,078 | | 42,078 |
| 37,544 | 37,544 | 39,222 |
| 24,532 | 39,222 | 37,544 |
| 39,222 | 39,222 > 37,544 | 24,532 |

Compare. Write > or < for each ◯.

**1.** 3,211 ◯ 4,221

**2.** 35,746 ◯ 35,645

**3.** 355,462 ◯ 535,845

**4.** Order the numbers from greatest to least. 62,500  62,721  63,001  61,435

_____ ; _____ ; _____ ; _____

**5. Number Sense** Write 3 numbers that are greater than 12,000, but less than 13,000.

_____

# Ordering Numbers

Compare. Write > or < for each ◯ .

**1.** 854,376 ◯ 845,763

**2.** 6,789 ◯ 9,876

**3.** 59,635 ◯ 59,536

**4.** 374,125 ◯ 743,225

Order the numbers from least to greatest.

**5.** 458,592   493,621   439,582

_____   _____   _____

**6. Number Sense** Write three numbers that are greater than 543,000 but less than 544,000.

_____   _____   _____

**7.** Put the states in order from the least populated to most populated state.

_____

_____

_____

_____

_____

**The Five Least Populated States**

| State | Population (2010) |
| --- | --- |
| Alaska | 721,523 |
| North Dakota | 675,905 |
| South Dakota | 819,761 |
| Vermont | 630,337 |
| Wyoming | 568,300 |

**8.** Which number has the greatest value?

**A** 865,437        **B** 826,911        **C** 853,812        **D** 862,391

**9. Writing to Explain** Tell how you could use a number line to determine which of two numbers is greater.

_____

_____

# Rounding Whole Numbers

Round 742,883 to the nearest thousand.

You can use place value or a number line to help you round numbers. On the number line below, 742,883 is between 742,000 and 743,000. The halfway number is 742,500.

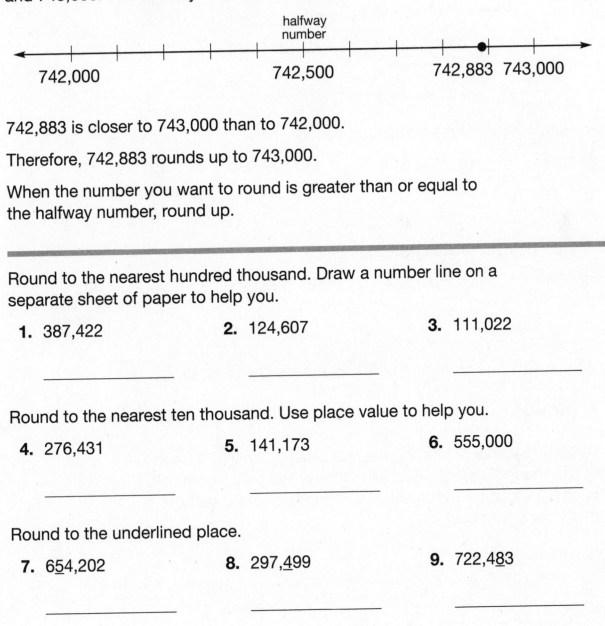

halfway
number

742,000          742,500          742,883   743,000

742,883 is closer to 743,000 than to 742,000.

Therefore, 742,883 rounds up to 743,000.

When the number you want to round is greater than or equal to the halfway number, round up.

Round to the nearest hundred thousand. Draw a number line on a separate sheet of paper to help you.

**1.** 387,422          **2.** 124,607          **3.** 111,022

_____          _____          _____

Round to the nearest ten thousand. Use place value to help you.

**4.** 276,431          **5.** 141,173          **6.** 555,000

_____          _____          _____

Round to the underlined place.

**7.** 6<u>5</u>4,202          **8.** 297,<u>4</u>99          **9.** 722,4<u>8</u>3

_____          _____          _____

Name _____

# Rounding Whole Numbers

Round each number to the nearest ten.

**1.** 16,326          **2.** 412,825          **3.** 512,162          **4.** 84,097

_____          _____          _____          _____

Round each number to the nearest hundred.

**5.** 1,427          **6.** 68,136          **7.** 271,308          **8.** 593,656

_____          _____          _____          _____

Round each number to the nearest thousand.

**9.** 18,366          **10.** 409,614          **11.** 229,930          **12.** 563,239

_____          _____          _____          _____

Round each number to the underlined place.

**13.** 12,108          **14.** 570,274          **15.** 333,625          **16.** 534,307

_____          _____          _____          _____

**17.** What is 681,542 rounded to the nearest hundred thousand?

**A** 600,000          **B** 680,000          **C** 700,000          **D** 780,000

**18. Writing to Explain** Mrs. Kennedy is buying pencils for each of 315 students at Hamilton Elementary. The pencils are sold in boxes of tens. How can she use rounding to decide how many pencils to buy?

_____

_____

_____

# Problem Solving:
# Make an Organized List

**Theme Park** Brian has four passes to a theme park. He could bring himself and three friends. The group of friends for him to choose from includes Art, Ned, Jeff, and Belinda. How many different combinations are possible?

## Read and Understand

**Step 1: What do you know?**

There are four friends: Art, Ned, Jeff, and Belinda.

**Step 2: What are you trying to find?**

Find out how many different combinations of friends Brian can take.

## Plan and Solve

**Step 3: What strategy will you use?**

**Strategy:** Make an Organized List

Brian, Art, Ned, Jeff, and Belinda. Brian has to be in each combination.

**List the choices:**
Brian, Art, Ned, Belinda
Brian, Art, Ned, Jeff
Brian, Art, Jeff, Belinda
Brian, Ned, Jeff, Belinda

**Answer:** There are four combinations.

## Look Back and Check

**Is your work correct?**

Yes, because each combination uses Brian. The way the list is organized shows that all ways were found.

Finish solving the problem.

1. Ann, Mara, Jenny, Tina, and Sue are sisters. Two of the five sisters must help their father at his business each Saturday. How many combinations of two sisters are possible?

   _____

   _____

Ann    Mara        Jenny   Tina
Ann    Jenny

Name _____

# Problem Solving:
# Make an Organized List

Make an organized list to solve each problem. Write each
answer in a complete sentence.

1.  Tonya and Lauren are designing a soccer uniform. They
    want to use two colors on the shirt. Their choices are
    green, orange, yellow, purple, blue, and silver. How many
    ways can they choose two colors?

    _____

    _____

    _____

2.  Yancey collects plastic banks. He has three different banks:
    a pig, a cow, and a horse. How many ways can Yancey
    arrange his banks on a shelf?

    _____

    _____

3.  Kevin has a rabbit, a ferret, a gerbil, and a turtle. He feeds
    them in a different order each day. In how many different
    orders can Kevin feed his pets?

    _____

    _____

    _____

    _____

# Using Mental Math to Add and Subtract

There are different strategies for adding and subtracting with mental math.

| **Addition Strategies** | | **Subtraction Strategies** | |
|---|---|---|---|
| With breaking apart you can add numbers in any order. | | Using compensation | |
| 235 + 158 | Break apart 158. 158 = 5 + 153 | 162 − 48 | Add 2 to make 50. 2 + 48 = 50 |
| 235 + 5 = 240 | Add one part to make a ten. | 162 − 50 = 112 | |
| 240 + 153 = 393 | Add the other part. | 112 + 2 = 114 | Since you subtracted 2 too many, add 2 to the answer. |
| With compensation you can add or subtract to make tens. | | Using counting on | |
| 235 + 158 | Add 2 to make a ten. 158 + 2 = 160 | 400 − 185 | Add 5 to make 190. 185 + 5 = 190 |
| 235 + 160 = 395 | | 190 + 10 = 200 | Make the next 100. |
| | | 200 + 200 = 400 | Add 200 to make 400. |
| 395 − 2 = 393 | Subtract 2 from the answer because 2 was added earlier. | 5 + 10 + 200 = 215 | Find the total of what you added. |

Add or subtract. Use mental math.

**1.** 67 + 31 = _____

**2.** 86 − 14 = _____

**3.** 29 + 43 = _____

**4.** 206 − 78 = _____

**5. Reasoning** How can you write 72 + (8 + 19) to make it easier to add? _____

| Marble Collection | |
|---|---|
| red | 425 |
| blue | 375 |
| green | 129 |
| yellow | 99 |

Use mental math to solve.

**6.** How many more blue marbles are there than yellow marbles? _____

**7.** What is the number of red and green marbles? _____

# Using Mental Math to Add and Subtract

Add or subtract. Use mental math.

**1.** $89 + 46$

_____

**2.** $101 - 49$

_____

**3.** $400 + 157$

_____

**4.** $722 + 158$

_____

**5.** $120 - 33$

_____

**6.** $900 - 187$

_____

**7.** $299 + 206$

_____

**8.** $878 + 534$

_____

**9.** $554 - 59$

_____

**10. Reasoning** How can you write $52 + (8 + 25)$ to make it easier to add? _____

**11.** Selena's family went on a trip. The total hotel bill was $659. The cost of the airfare was $633. Use mental math to find the total cost for the hotel and the airfare. _____

**12.** One year, 76 people helped at the town cleanup. The next year, 302 people helped. How many more people helped in the second year? Use mental math to find the answer. _____

**13.** Stanley wants to collect 900 sports cards. So far, he has collected 428 baseball cards and 217 football cards. How many more cards does Stanley need to complete his collection?

**A** 255      **B** 472      **C** 645      **D** 683

**14. Writing to Explain** Explain how you could add $678 + 303$ using mental math.

_____

_____

_____

# Estimating Sums and Differences of Whole Numbers

Rounding can be used to estimate sums and differences.

To estimate 1,436 + 422:

**Rounding**

1,436  rounds to 1,400
422     rounds to 400
1,400 + 400 = 1,800

To estimate 3,635 − 1,498:

**Rounding**

3,635  rounds to 3,600
1,498  rounds to 1,500
3,600 − 1,500 = 2,100

Estimate each sum or difference.

1. 265
   + 426

2. 348
   + 122

3. 562
   − 223

4. 824
   − 590

5. 2,189
   + 388

6. 1,329
   + 5,345

7. 877
   − 475

8. 9,245
   − 4,033

9. 788 + 212 = _____

10. 9,769 − 4,879 = _____

11. 65,328 − 14,231 = _____

12. 32,910 + 4,085 = _____

13. **Number Sense** Is 976 − 522 more or less than 400? Explain how you can tell without actually subtracting.

_____

14. The fourth graders are helping raise money for the local animal shelter. They hoped to raise $1,000. So far they have made $465 in bake sales and $710 in T-shirt sales. About how much more than $1,000 have they raised? _____

Name _____

# Estimating Sums and Differences of Whole Numbers

Estimate each sum or difference.

1.  627
    + 95

2.  829
    − 292

3.  987
    − 233

4.  1,568
    + 352

5. 4,263 − 1,613 _____

6. 7,502 + 2,187 _____

7. 24,141 − 2,177 _____

8. 64,099 − 55,555 _____

9. 83,595 + 18,999 _____

10. About how much larger is the largest ocean than the smallest ocean?

    _____

    _____

    _____

**Ocean Area**

| Ocean | Area (million sq km) |
|---|---|
| Arctic Ocean | 14,056 |
| Atlantic Ocean | 76,762 |
| Indian Ocean | 68,556 |
| Pacific Ocean | 155,557 |

11. About how many million square kilometers do all the oceans together cover?

    _____

12. Mallory is a pilot. Last week she flew the following round trips in miles: 2,020; 1,358; 952; 2,258; and 1,888. Which of the following is a good estimate of the miles Mallory flew last week?

    **A** 6,000 mi      **B** 6,800 mi      **C** 7,000 mi      **D** 8,000 mi

13. **Writing to Explain** Explain how you would estimate to subtract 189 from 643.

    _____

    _____

# Adding Whole Numbers

You can add more than two numbers when you line up the numbers by place value and add one place at a time.

Add 3,456 + 139 + 5,547.

Estimate: 3,000 + 100 + 6,000 = 9,100

| **Step 1** | **Step 2** | **Step 3** |
|---|---|---|
| Line up numbers by place value. | Add the tens. | Add the hundreds, then the thousands. |
| Add the ones. | Regroup if needed. | Continue to regroup. |
| Regroup if needed. | | |

**Step 1**

$$\begin{array}{r} {\scriptstyle 2} \\ 3,456 \\ 139 \\ + 5,547 \\ \hline 2 \end{array}$$

22 becomes 2 tens and 2 ones.

**Step 2**

$$\begin{array}{r} {\scriptstyle 1\,2} \\ 3,456 \\ 139 \\ + 5,547 \\ \hline 42 \end{array}$$

Keep digits in neat columns as you add.

**Step 3**

$$\begin{array}{r} {\scriptstyle 1\ 1\,2} \\ 3,456 \\ 139 \\ + 5,547 \\ \hline 9,142 \end{array}$$

9,142 is close to the estimate of 9,100.

Add.

1.  $\begin{array}{r} 945 \\ 124 \\ + 343 \\ \hline \end{array}$

2.  $\begin{array}{r} 2,588 \\ 373 \\ + 866 \\ \hline \end{array}$

3.  $\begin{array}{r} 12,566 \\ 8,222 \\ + 5,532 \\ \hline \end{array}$

4.  $\begin{array}{r} 2,955 \\ 9,017 \\ + 248 \\ \hline \end{array}$

5.  $\begin{array}{r} 16,699 \\ 3,311 \\ + 32,484 \\ \hline \end{array}$

6.  $\begin{array}{r} 3,881 \\ 1,735 \\ + 364 \\ \hline \end{array}$

7. **Number Sense** Jill added 450 + 790 + 123 and got 1,163. Is this sum reasonable?

_____

_____

Name _____

# Adding Whole Numbers

Add.

1.  486
    875
    + 45

2.  4,334
    4,948
    + 890

3.    938
    1,487
    + 8,947

4.   7,226
     1,587
    + 72,984

5.  54,236
       223
    + 7,856

6.     80
      960
        4
    + 1,986

7.  27,987
     2,096
    15,098
    + 7,945

8.  8,738
    5,234
      836
    + 237

9. **Number Sense** Luke added 429 + 699 + 314 and got 950. Is this sum reasonable?

_____

10. What is the combined length of the three longest glaciers?

_____

11. What is the total combined length of the four longest glaciers in the world?

### World's Longest Glaciers

| Glacier | Length (miles) |
|---|---|
| Lambert-Fisher Ice Passage | 320 |
| Novaya Zemlya | 260 |
| Arctic Institute Ice Passage | 225 |
| Nimrod-Lennox-King | 180 |

_____

12. Which is the sum of 3,774 + 8,276 + 102?

   **A** 1,251     **B** 12,152     **C** 13,052     **D** 102,152

13. **Writing to Explain** Leona added 6,641 + 1,482 + 9,879. Should her answer be more than or less than 15,000?

_____

Name _____

# Subtracting Whole Numbers

Here is how to subtract.

Find 7,445 − 1,368.

Estimate: 7,000 − 1,000 = 6,000

| **Step 1** | **Step 2** | **Step 3** | **Step 4** |
|---|---|---|---|
| 315<br>7,44̶5̶<br>− 1,368<br>———<br>7 | 13<br>3 ̶8̶15<br>7,44̶5̶<br>− 1,368<br>———<br>77 | 13<br>3 ̶8̶15<br>7,44̶5̶<br>− 1,368<br>———<br>077 | 13<br>3 ̶8̶15<br>7,44̶5̶<br>− 1,368<br>———<br>6,077 |
| You cannot subtract 8 ones from 5 ones. You must regroup.<br><br>Regroup 4 tens as 3 tens and 10 ones.<br><br>Subtract 8 ones from 15 ones. | You cannot subtract 6 tens from 3 tens. You must regroup.<br><br>Regroup 4 hundreds as 3 hundreds and 10 tens.<br><br>Subtract 6 tens from 13 tens. | Subtract 3 hundreds from 3 hundreds. | Subtract 1 thousand from 7 thousands.<br><br>1 1<br>6,077<br>+ 1,368<br>———<br>7,445<br><br>You can check your answer using addition. |

Subtract.

1.    624
     − 379

2.    759
     − 211

3.    814
     − 662

4.    391
     − 208

5.   4,772
     −1,671

6.   8,335
     − 4,188

7.   4,219
     − 1,379

8.   5,216
     − 2,158

9. **Estimation** Carlos has 2,175 marbles in his collection. Emily has 1,833 marbles in her collection. Carlos says that he has about 1,000 more marbles than Emily. Is Carlos correct?

_____

_____

**R 4·4**

Name _____

# Subtracting Whole Numbers

Subtract.

1.  7,242
    − 158

2.  520
    − 203

3.  848
    − 257

4.  6,797
    − 1,298

5.  753
    − 218

6.  7,392
    − 4,597

7.  3,898
    − 1,299

8.  3,721
    − 459

**9.** 3,328 − 1,754          **10.** 9,333 − 1,555          **11.** 6,797 − 1,298

**12.** Which of the following best describes the answer to the subtraction problem below?

$$3,775 − 1,831$$

A  The answer is less than 1,000.

B  The answer is about 1,000.

C  The answer is greater than 1,000.

D  You cannot tell from the information given.

**13. Writing to Explain** The Environmental Club's goal is to collect 1,525 cans by the end of the summer. The number of cans they collected each week is shown in the table below. How can you find the number of cans they need to collect in week 4 to meet their goal?

| Week Number | Number of cans collected |
| --- | --- |
| 1 | 378 |
| 2 | 521 |
| 3 | 339 |
| 4 | |

_____

_____

# Subtracting Across Zeros

Here is how to subtract across zeros.

Find $606 - 377$.

Estimate: $600 - 400 = 200$

| Step 1 | Step 2 | Step 3 | Step 4 |
|---|---|---|---|
| $\begin{array}{r} 606 \\ -\ 377 \\ \hline \end{array}$ | $\begin{array}{r} {}^{5\ 10} \\ \cancel{606} \\ -\ 377 \\ \hline \end{array}$ | $\begin{array}{r} {}^{9} \\ {}^{5\ \cancel{10}\ 16} \\ \cancel{606} \\ -\ 377 \\ \hline \end{array}$ | $\begin{array}{r} {}^{9} \\ {}^{5\ \cancel{10}\ 16} \\ \cancel{606} \\ -\ 377 \\ \hline 229 \end{array}$ |
| You cannot subtract 7 ones from 6 ones, so you must regroup. | Since there is a zero in the tens place, you must regroup using the hundreds. Regroup 6 hundreds as 5 hundreds and 10 tens. | Regroup 10 tens and 6 ones as 9 tens and 16 ones. | Subtract. $\begin{array}{r} {}^{1\ 1} \\ 229 \\ +\ 377 \\ \hline 606 \end{array}$ You can check your answer by using addition. |

Subtract.

1. $\begin{array}{r} 707 \\ -\ \ 58 \\ \hline \end{array}$
2. $\begin{array}{r} 950 \\ -\ \ 47 \\ \hline \end{array}$
3. $\begin{array}{r} 800 \\ -\ 638 \\ \hline \end{array}$
4. $\begin{array}{r} 3{,}506 \\ -\ \ 866 \\ \hline \end{array}$

5. $\begin{array}{r} 4{,}507 \\ -\ 3{,}569 \\ \hline \end{array}$
6. $\begin{array}{r} 3{,}076 \\ -\ 1{,}466 \\ \hline \end{array}$
7. $\begin{array}{r} 8{,}106 \\ -\ 2{,}999 \\ \hline \end{array}$
8. $\begin{array}{r} 6{,}083 \\ -\ 1{,}492 \\ \hline \end{array}$

9. **Reasonableness** Lexi subtracts 9,405 from 11,138. Should her answer be greater than or less than 2,000? Explain.

_____

_____

# Subtracting Across Zeros

Subtract.

1.    906
  –   45

2.    3,091
  – 1,361

3.    4,000
  – 2,557

4.     800
  –   139

5.    1,070
  –   593

6.    8,904
  – 3,596

7.    3,007
  – 2,366

8.     523
  – 203

9. $7,403 - 3,254$

10. $5,067 - 2,987$

11. $6,790 - 1,298$

_____     _____     _____

12. Robert set a goal to swim 1,000 laps in the local swimming pool during his summer break. Robert has currently finished 642 laps. How many more laps does he have to swim in order to meet his goal?

    **A**   332       **B**   358       **C**   468       **D**   472

13. **Writing to Explain** If $694 - 72 =$ _____, then $622 +$ _____ $= 694$. Explain the process of checking your work.

_____

_____

_____

_____

# Problem Solving: Draw a Picture and Write an Equation

Read the question and follow the steps to develop a problem-solving strategy.

In the morning, a grocery store had 28 apples on display. By the end of the day, 11 apples had been purchased. How many apples were left?

**Step 1: Read/Understand**

- Find the information you are given. [There were 28 apples; now there are 11 fewer apples.]

- Find the information you need to figure out. [The number of apples that are left]

**Step 2: Plan**

- Draw a picture that helps you visualize the problem you are trying to solve.

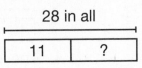

28 in all

| 11 | ? |

**Step 3: Solve**

- Figure out which operation you need to use to solve the problem, and write an equation. [Subtraction; 28 − 11 = ?]

- Solve the equation to answer the problem. [28 − 11 = 17; 17 apples were left.]

---

1. **Strategy Practice** On Monday, Erika put 12 flakes of fish food in her fish tank before school, and 13 more when she got home. How many flakes did she put in the tank that day? Use the steps to answer the question. _____

**Step 1:**

- What information are you given?

- What information do you need to figure out?

**Step 2:**

- Draw a picture.

**Step 3:**

- Choose an operation and write an equation.

- Solve the equation.

Solve the following problems. Draw pictures to help you.

2. Roy is reading a book that is 68 pages. He has read 24 pages so far. How many more pages does he have to read to finish the book? _____

3. There are 29 students in the school band. During practice, 6 new students joined the band. How many students are in the band now? _____

4. Jaycee's teacher gave her a box of 96 pens. She gave 17 of the pens to her classmates. How many pens were left in the box? _____

Name _____

# Problem Solving: Draw a Picture and Write an Equation

For exercises **1** through **4** write an equation and solve. Use the picture to help you.

**1.** A remote control car has a speed of 5 feet per second. How many feet will the car travel in 6 seconds?

_____

? feet in 6 seconds

| 5 ft | 5 ft | 5 ft | 5 ft | 5 ft | 5 ft |
|------|------|------|------|------|------|

**2.** Danny has 45 minutes to take a math test. If Danny finishes half the test in 19 minutes, how many minutes does he have left to finish it?

_____

45 minutes

| 19 minutes | ? minutes left |
|------------|----------------|

**3.** While shopping, Janet bought a shirt for $8, a pair of jeans for $22, mittens for $5, and a hat for $10. How much money did Janet spend?

_____

? money spent

| $8 | $22 | $5 | $10 |
|----|-----|----|----|

**4.** The 175th anniversary of the completion of the Erie Canal was in the year 2000. If it took 8 years to dig the canal, in what year did the digging of the Erie Canal begin?

_____

Year 2000

| 175 | 8 | ? year digging began |
|-----|---|----------------------|

**5.** The average length of a song on a certain CD is 3 minutes. The CD has 12 songs. Write an equation for the length of the whole CD. Draw a picture to help you.

**A** $12 \times 3$          **B** $12 + 3$          **C** $12 \div 3$          **D** $12 - 3$

**6. Writing to Explain** It takes Jinny 56 minutes to drive to her friend's house. She drove 15 minutes and then stopped at a store. She then drove another 10 minutes. What do you need to do to find the amount of time she has left to drive?

_____

_____

_____

P 4•6

# Arrays and Multiplying by 10 and 100

You can use addition to help you multiply.

**Find 3 × 10.**

There are three groups of 10.

Add 10 three times
10 + 10 + 10 = 30
    or
Multiply 3 groups of 10.
3 × 10 = 30

**Find 3 × 100.**

There are three groups of 100.

Add 100 three times.
100 + 100 + 100 = 300
    or
Multiply 3 groups of 100.
3 × 100 = 300

Find each product.

**1.** Find 4 × 10.

Add: 10 + 10 + 10 + 10 = _____

So, 4 × 10 = _____.

**2.** Find 2 × 100.

Add: 100 + 100 = _____

So, 2 × 100 = _____.

**3. Reasonableness** Michael used addition to find 9 × 100 and he said the product was 90. What did he do wrong?

_____

**4.** Draw two sets of arrays to represent 6 × 10 and 5 × 100. Then show how to use addition to find each product.

# Arrays and Multiplying by 10 and 100

Find each product.

**1.** $5 \times 10 =$ _____

**2.** $2 \times 100 =$ _____

**3.** $3 \times 10 =$ _____

**4.** $3 \times 100 =$ _____

**5.** $6 \times 10 =$ _____

**6.** $5 \times 100 =$ _____

**7. Reasoning** What whole number could you use to complete
☐ $\times 100 =$ ☐00 so that ☐00 is greater than 400 but less than 600?

_____

**8.** Mr. James does 100 sit-ups every morning. How many sit-ups will he do in 7 days?

**A** 70      **B** 100      **C** 107      **D** 700

**9. Writing to Explain** Jackie has 10 groups of pennies with 3 pennies in each group. Carlos has 5 groups of pennies with 100 pennies in each group. Who has more pennies? Explain how you know.

_____

_____

_____

_____

# Multiplying by Multiples of 10 and 100

Patterns can help you multiply by numbers that are multiples of 10 or 100.

$3 \times 5 = 15$         $2 \times 4 = 8$         $5 \times 7 = 35$

$3 \times 50 = 150$       $2 \times 40 = 80$      $5 \times 70 = 350$

$3 \times 500 = 1,500$    $2 \times 400 = 800$    $5 \times 700 = 3,500$

To find each of the products above, first complete the basic multiplication fact. Then write the same number of zeros seen in the factor that is a multiple of 10. If the product ends in a zero, the answer will have an extra zero. For example:

Find $4 \times 500$.

First find $4 \times 5$.                              $4 \times 5 = 20$

Then, count the number of zeros
in the multiple of 100.                              **500 has 2 zeros.**

Write 2 zeros after the product
of the basic multiplication fact.
So, there are 3 zeros in the product.   **2,000**

Find each product. Use mental math.

**1.** $8 \times 80 =$ _____   **2.** $6 \times 60 =$ _____

**3.** $7 \times 90 =$ _____   **4.** $5 \times 200 =$ _____

**5.** $3 \times 40 =$ _____   **6.** $7 \times 200 =$ _____

**7.** $500 \times 6 =$ _____   **8.** $600 \times 9 =$ _____

**9.** $3 \times 800 =$ _____   **10.** $600 \times 7 =$ _____

**11. Number Sense** To find $8 \times 600$, multiply 8 and 6, then write ___ zeros to form the product.

R 5·2

# Multiplying by Multiples of 10 and 100

Find each product. Use mental math.

**1.** $6 \times 70 =$ _____

**2.** $80 \times 2 =$ _____

**3.** $40 \times 9 =$ _____

**4.** $20 \times 3 =$ _____

**5.** $4 \times 500 =$ _____

**6.** $300 \times 9 =$ _____

**7.** $8 \times 600 =$ _____

**8.** $7 \times 400 =$ _____

**9.** $6 \times 200 =$ _____

**10.** $800 \times 5 =$ _____

**11.** $6 \times 800 =$ _____

**12.** $400 \times 3 =$ _____

**13. Number Sense** How many zeros will the product of $7 \times 500$ have? _____

Mr. Young has 30 times as many pencils as Jack. The whole school has 200 times as many pencils as Jack. If Jack has 2 pencils, how many pencils do the following have?

**14.** Mr. Young?

**15.** The whole school?

_____

_____

**16.** Find $3 \times 400$.

  **A** 120     **B** 1,200     **C** 12,000     **D** 120,000

**17. Writing to Explain** Wendi says that the product of $5 \times 400$ will have 2 zeros. Is she correct? Explain.

_____

_____

_____

# Breaking Apart to Multiply

You can make multiplication easier by breaking larger numbers apart by place value.

Find 3 × 35.

Break apart 35 into 30 + 5.

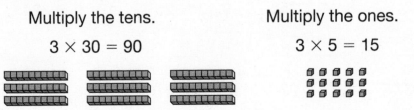

Multiply the tens.

3 × 30 = 90

Multiply the ones.

3 × 5 = 15

Add the partial products: 90 + 15 = 105

So, 3 × 35 = 105.

Complete.

**1.** 5 × 23

5 × 20 = ☐

5 × 3 = ☐

☐ + ☐ = ☐

**2.** 4 × 246

4 × 200 = ☐

4 × 40 = ☐

4 × 6 = ☐

☐ + ☐ + ☐ = ☐

Find each product. You may use place-value blocks or drawings to help.

**3.** 6 × 21 = _____

**4.** 5 × 43 = _____

**5.** 3 × 116 = _____

**6.** 5 × 22 = _____

**7.** 3 × 352 = _____

**8.** 7 × 226 = _____

**9.** 4 × 34 = _____

**10.** 6 × 217 = _____

**11. Number Sense** Tim said, "To find 6 × 33, I can add 18 + 18."
Do you agree with Tim? Why or why not?

_____

Name _____

# Breaking Apart to Multiply

Find each product. You may use place-value blocks or draw a picture to help.

**1.** 4 × 43     **2.** 7 × 218     **3.** 5 × 13     **4.** 2 × 88     **5.** 4 × 334

_____    _____    _____    _____    _____

**6.** 3 × 49     **7.** 6 × 42     **8.** 4 × 156     **9.** 3 × 25     **10.** 5 × 224

_____    _____    _____    _____    _____

**11.** 2 × 54     **12.** 4 × 337     **13.** 7 × 22     **14.** 5 × 216     **15.** 6 × 137

_____    _____    _____    _____    _____

**16.** A carpenter makes chairs with slats that run across the back of the chairs as shown. Each chair uses 7 slats. He needs to make 24 chairs. How many slats must he make?

Slats

_____

**17.** Each wood panel is 6 feet wide. Exactly 19 panels are needed to cover the walls of a room. How many feet of wood panels are needed?

_____

**18.** Which is equal to 5 × 25?

   **A** (5 × 5) + (2 × 5)       **C** 5 × 20

   **B** (5 × 20) + (5 × 1)     **D** (5 × 20) + (5 × 5)

**19. Writing to Explain** How can you multiply 242 × 8 by breaking apart numbers?

_____

_____

_____

Name _____

# Using Mental Math to Multiply

You can multiply mentally by using compensation.

Find 4 × 19 using compensation.

**Step 1:** Substitute a number for 19 that is easy to multiply by 4.

$$4 \times 19$$
$$\downarrow \qquad \text{Add 1 to make 20.}$$
$$4 \times 20$$

**Step 2:** Find the new product.

$$4 \times 20 = 80$$

**Step 3:** Now adjust. Subtract 4 groups of 1.

$$80 - 4 = 76$$

So, 4 × 19 = 76.

Find 6 × 205 using compensation.

**Step 1:** Substitute a number for 205 that is easy to multiply by 6.

$$6 \times 205$$
$$\downarrow \qquad \text{Subtract 5}$$
$$6 \times 200 \qquad \text{to make 200.}$$

**Step 2:** Find the new product.

$$6 \times 200 = 1,200$$

**Step 3:** Now adjust. Add 6 groups of 5.

$$1,200 + 30 = 1,230$$

So, 6 × 205 = 1,230.

Use compensation to find each product.

**1.** 5 × 32 = _____

**2.** 195 × 5 = _____

**3.** 7 × 53 = _____

**4.** 66 × 2 = _____

**5.** 6 × 497 = _____

**6.** 92 × 4 = _____

**7.** 603 × 3 = _____

**8.** 31 × 8 = _____

**9.** 598 × 5 = _____

**10.** 4 × 29 = _____

**11.** 4 × 199 = _____

**12.** 310 × 6 = _____

**13. Algebra** In $a \times 60 = 120$, $a$ is a one-digit number. What number does $a$ represent?

_____

Name _____

# Using Mental Math to Multiply

Use compensation to find each product.

**1.** 34 × 4 = _____     **2.** 199 × 6 = _____     **3.** 53 × 7 = _____

**4.** 505 × 4 = _____     **5.** 41 × 6 = _____     **6.** 298 × 6 = _____

**7.** 76 × 5 = _____     **8.** 803 × 7 = _____     **9.** 83 × 3 = _____

**10.** 390 × 2 = _____     **11.** 28 × 8 = _____     **12.** 709 × 4 = _____

**13.** 94 × 2 = _____     **14.** 410 × 8 = _____     **15.** 16 × 4 = _____

**16.** 197 × 5 = _____     **17.** 46 × 5 = _____     **18.** 896 × 9 = _____

**19. Reasonableness** Quinn used compensation to find the product of 37 × 4. First, she found 40 × 4 = 160. Then she adjusted that product by adding 3 groups of 4 to get her final answer of 172. What did she do incorrectly?

_____

_____

_____

**20.** Davidson's Bakery uses 9 dozen eggs to make cookies each day. There are twelve eggs in one dozen. How many eggs do they use?

**A** 90     **B** 98     **C** 108     **D** 112

**21. Writing to Explain** Find the product of 503 × 6. Explain how you found the product.

_____

_____

_____

# Using Rounding to Estimate

You can use rounding to estimate products.

Use rounding to estimate 7 × 28.

First, round 28 to the nearest ten.
  28 rounds to 30.

Then, multiply.
  7 × 30 = 210

So, 7 × 28 is about 210.

Use rounding to estimate 7 × 215.

First, round 215 to the nearest hundred.
  215 rounds to 200.

Then, multiply.
  7 × 200 = 1,400

So, 7 × 215 is about 1,400.

Estimate each product.

**1.** 6 × 88 is close to 6 × _____

**2.** 279 × 4 is close to _____ × 4

**3.** 7 × 31 _____

**4.** 38 × 5 _____

**5.** 21 × 6 _____

**6.** 3 × 473 _____

**7.** 5 × 790 _____

**8.** 488 × 6 _____

**9. Number Sense** Estimate to determine if 5 × 68 is greater
than or less than 350. Tell how you decided.

_____

_____

**10.** Estimate how many of Part C
would be made in 4 months.

_____

**11.** Estimate how many of Part B
would be made in 3 months.

_____

**12.** Estimate how many of Part A
would be made in 9 months.

_____

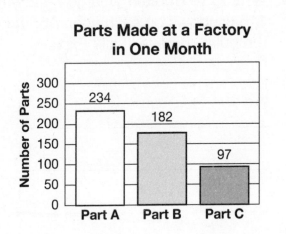

**Parts Made at a Factory
in One Month**

Number of Parts: 234 (Part A), 182 (Part B), 97 (Part C)

# Using Rounding to Estimate

Estimate each product.

**1.** 38 × 2 _____

**2.** 7 × 47 _____

**3.** 54 × 6 _____

**4.** 121 × 2 _____

**5.** 578 × 8 _____

**6.** 823 × 3 _____

**7.** 7 × 289 _____

**8.** 183 × 4 _____

**9.** 2 × 87 _____

**10.** 673 × 8 _____

The distance between Bill's house and his aunt's house
is 835 miles.

**11.** About how many miles would
he drive if he made 4 one-way
trips?

**12.** About how many miles would
he drive if he made 9 one-way trips?

_____

_____

**13.** Vera has 8 boxes of paper clips. Each box contains
275 paper clips. About how many paper clips does Vera have?

**A** 240          **B** 1,600          **C** 2,400          **D** 24,000

**14.** **Writing to Explain** A large 7-story office building has
116 windows on each floor. About how many windows does
the building have in all? Explain.

_____

_____

_____

_____

# Problem Solving: Reasonableness

After you solve a problem, it is important to check your answer to see whether it is reasonable.

**Read and Understand**   There are 5 animals on a farm. Each animal eats 105 pounds of food per week. How much food does the farmer have to buy each week?

? pounds of food in all

| 105 | 105 | 105 | 105 | 105 |

**Plan and Solve**   Use breaking apart or compensation to find $5 \times 105$.
$5 \times 105 = 525$

**Check for Reasonableness**   First, ask yourself, "Did I answer the right question?" Then, estimate to check your answer. $5 \times 100 = 500$. The answer is reasonable because 500 is close to 525.

Solve the following problems. Check your answers for reasonableness.

1. Marisa says $302 \times 6 = 192$.
   Explain why Marisa's answer is not reasonable.

   _____

   _____

   _____

2. Jaime practiced swimming for about 11 hours every week for 8 weeks. About how many hours did he practice in all? How can you check your answer?

   _____

   _____

   _____

# Problem Solving: Reasonableness

For **1** and **2**, use reasonableness to decide if each answer is correct. Explain why the answer is reasonable or not. If the answer is incorrect, give the correct answer.

1. Johan is selling baseball cards for 12¢ each. He is selling 8 cards and says he'll make $8.

   _____

   _____

2. Erika wants to give 5 stickers to everyone in her class. Her class sits in 4 rows of 7, and Erika says she'll need 140 stickers.

   _____

   _____

3. Viktor has 7 piles of coins with 63 coins in each. Which is a reasonable number of coins in Viktor's piles?

   **A** 300, because 7 × 63 is about 7 × 40 = 280.

   **B** 360, because 7 × 63 is about 7 × 50 = 350.

   **C** 441, because 7 × 63 is about 7 × 60 = 420.

   **D** 500, because 7 × 63 is about 7 × 70 = 490.

Julie planted a sunflower and kept track of its height in a table. Use the table to solve **4** and **5**.

4. How tall will the sunflower be after the 5th week if it continues to grow at the same rate?

   _____

5. **Writing to Explain** The world's largest sunflower was about 300 inches tall. Julie says her sunflower will be that tall after 3 months. Is Julie's answer reasonable? Explain why or why not. (Remember, there are about 4 weeks in one month.)

   _____

   _____

| Height of Sunflower | |
|---|---|
| **Week** | **Height in Inches** |
| 1 | 16 |
| 2 | 32 |
| 3 | 48 |
| 4 | 64 |
| 5 | |

# Arrays and Using an Expanded Algorithm

You can use arrays of place-value blocks to multiply.

Find the product for $3 \times 14$.

| What You Show | What You Write |
|---|---|
| $3 \times 10 = 30$   $3 \times 4 = 12$<br><br>$30 + 12 = 42$ | $\begin{array}{r} 14 \\ \times\ \ 3 \\ \hline 12 \\ +\ 30 \\ \hline 42 \end{array}$   $\begin{array}{l} 3 \times 4 \text{ ones} \\ 3 \times 1 \text{ ten} \end{array}$ |

Draw an array for each problem to find the partial products and the product. Complete the calculation.

1. $\begin{array}{r} 18 \\ \times\ \ 4 \\ \hline \end{array}$

2. $\begin{array}{r} 21 \\ \times\ \ 6 \\ \hline \end{array}$

3. $\begin{array}{r} 17 \\ \times\ \ 6 \\ \hline \end{array}$

4. $\begin{array}{r} 11 \\ \times\ \ 2 \\ \hline \end{array}$

5. $\begin{array}{r} 23 \\ \times\ \ 5 \\ \hline \end{array}$

6. $\begin{array}{r} 16 \\ \times\ \ 3 \\ \hline \end{array}$

7. **Number Sense** What two simpler problems can you use to find $9 \times 38$? (Hint: Think about the tens and ones.)

_____

# Arrays and Using an Expanded Algorithm

Use the array to find the partial products. Add the partial products to find the product.

**1.**   42
 × 8

**2.**   39
 × 7

**3.**   21
 × 4

**4.**   27
 × 6

**5.** $7 \times 14 =$ _____

**6.** $3 \times 52 =$ _____

**7.** $4 \times 42 =$ _____

**8.** $5 \times 26 =$ _____

**9.** $6 \times 62 =$ _____

**10.** $9 \times 76 =$ _____

**11.** Alex can type 72 words per minute. How many words can Alex type in 5 minutes?   _____

**12.** Find $8 \times 44$.

**A** 282          **B** 312          **C** 352          **D** 372

**13. Writing to Explain** Explain how you can use an array to find partial products for $4 \times 36$.

_____

_____

_____

Name _____

# Connecting the Expanded and Standard Algorithms

There are different ways to find the product for $3 \times 45$.

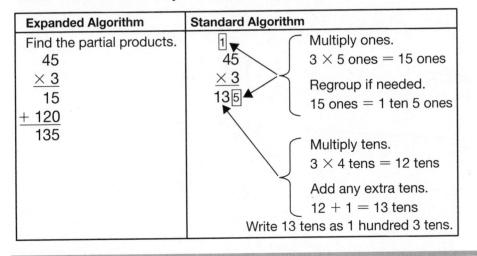

| Expanded Algorithm | Standard Algorithm |
|---|---|
| Find the partial products.<br><br>$\begin{array}{r} 45 \\ \times\ 3 \\ \hline 15 \\ +\ 120 \\ \hline 135 \end{array}$ | $\begin{array}{r} \boxed{1} \\ 45 \\ \times\ 3 \\ \hline 13\boxed{5} \end{array}$    Multiply ones.<br>$3 \times 5$ ones $= 15$ ones<br><br>Regroup if needed.<br>15 ones $= 1$ ten 5 ones<br><br>Multiply tens.<br>$3 \times 4$ tens $= 12$ tens<br><br>Add any extra tens.<br>$12 + 1 = 13$ tens<br>Write 13 tens as 1 hundred 3 tens. |

Solve.

1. **Draw a Picture** Find $4 \times 35$ using the expanded algorithm and then the standard algorithm.

2. At his job, Mr. Miller works 7 hours a day, Monday through Friday. How many hours does he work in 2 weeks?

   _____

3. **Think About the Process** Write the multiplication problem that matches the picture below. Then use the standard algorithm to find the product.

4. **Writing to Explain** Stella used the expanded algorithm to find the product for $9 \times 39$. Her work is shown below. Is she correct? Explain.

   $\begin{array}{r} 39 \\ \times\ 9 \\ \hline 270 \\ +\ 81 \\ \hline 351 \end{array}$    _____

   _____

   _____

Name _____

# Connecting the Expanded and Standard Algorithms

For **1** through **4**, use the expanded algorithm to multiply.

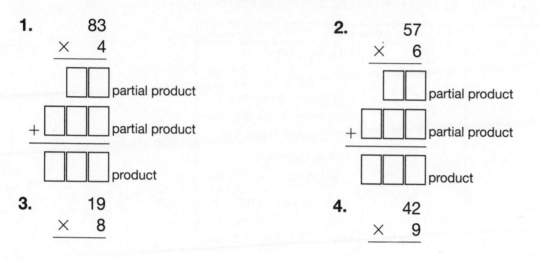

**1.**   83
     ×   4

     ☐☐  partial product
   + ☐☐☐  partial product
     ☐☐☐  product

**2.**   57
     ×   6

     ☐☐  partial product
   + ☐☐☐  partial product
     ☐☐☐  product

**3.**   19
     ×   8

**4.**   42
     ×   9

For **5** through **10**, use the standard algorithm to multiply.

**5.**    75
      ×   6

**6.**    64
      ×   5

**7.**    17
      ×   9

**8.**    93
      ×   4

**9.**    28
      ×   7

**10.**    56
       ×   8

**11.** A commuter van has 38 seats and 14 windows. How many windows are in 6 commuter vans?

   **A** 70          **B** 84          **C** 102          **D** 228

**12. Writing to Explain** Suppose you had to find 4 × 57. How are the expanded algorithm and the standard algorithm alike? How are they different?

_____

_____

_____

_____

# Multiplying 2-Digit by 1-Digit Numbers

Here is how to multiply a 2-digit number by a 1-digit number using paper and pencil.

| Find 3 × 24. | **What You Think** | **What You Write** |
|---|---|---|
| **Step 1**<br>Multiply the ones.<br>Regroup if necessary. | 3 × 4 = 12 ones<br>Regroup 12 ones as 1 ten 2 ones. | 1<br>24<br>× 3<br>2 |
| **Step 2**<br>Multiply the tens.<br>Add any extra tens. | 3 × 2 tens = 6 tens<br>6 tens + 1 ten = 7 tens | 1<br>24<br>× 3<br>72 |

Is your answer reasonable?

   Exact answer: 3 × 24 = 72

   Think: 24 is close to 25.

   Estimate: 3 × 25 = 75     Since 72 is close to 75, the answer is reasonable.

Find each product. Estimate to check reasonableness.

1.    13
    × 3

2.    17
    × 7

3.    24
    × 5

4.    48
    × 8

5.    62
    × 6

6.    36
    × 5

7.    88
    × 5

8.    52
    × 8

9. **Estimation** Use estimation to decide which has the greater product: 81 × 6 or 79 × 5.   _____

Name _____

# Multiplying 2-Digit by 1-Digit Numbers

Find each product. Estimate to check reasonableness.

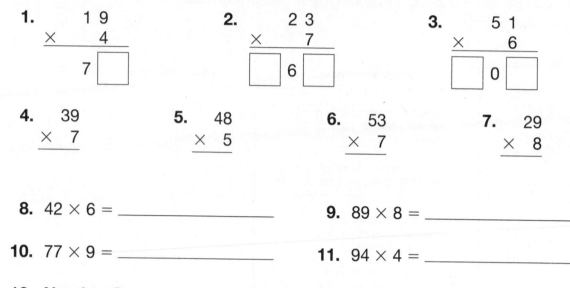

**1.**
$$\begin{array}{r} 1\,9 \\ \times \quad 4 \\ \hline 7\ \square \end{array}$$

**2.**
$$\begin{array}{r} 2\,3 \\ \times \quad 7 \\ \hline \square\,6\,\square \end{array}$$

**3.**
$$\begin{array}{r} 5\,1 \\ \times \quad 6 \\ \hline \square\,0\,\square \end{array}$$

**4.**
$$\begin{array}{r} 39 \\ \times \ 7 \\ \hline \end{array}$$

**5.**
$$\begin{array}{r} 48 \\ \times \ 5 \\ \hline \end{array}$$

**6.**
$$\begin{array}{r} 53 \\ \times \ 7 \\ \hline \end{array}$$

**7.**
$$\begin{array}{r} 29 \\ \times \ 8 \\ \hline \end{array}$$

**8.** $42 \times 6 =$ _____

**9.** $89 \times 8 =$ _____

**10.** $77 \times 9 =$ _____

**11.** $94 \times 4 =$ _____

**12. Number Sense** Penny says that $4 \times 65 = 260$. Estimate to check Penny's answer. Is she right? Explain.

_____

_____

**13.** A large dump truck uses about 18 gallons of fuel for 1 hour of work. About how many gallons of fuel are needed if the truck works for 5 hours?

_____

**14.** Which of the following is a reasonable estimate for $6 \times 82$?

**A** 48      **B** 480      **C** 540      **D** 550

**15. Writing to Explain** Tyrone has 6 times as many marbles as his sister Pam. Pam has 34 marbles. Louis has 202 marbles. Who has more marbles, Tyrone or Louis? Explain how you found your answer.

_____

_____

# Multiplying 3- and 4-Digit by 1-Digit Numbers

The steps below show how to multiply greater numbers.

|  | Example A | Example B |
|---|---|---|
| **Step 1**<br>Multiply the ones.<br>Regroup if necessary. | 1<br>154<br>× 4<br>—<br>6 | 2<br>1,214<br>× 7<br>—<br>8 |
| **Step 2**<br>Multiply the tens.<br>Add any extra tens.<br>Regroup if necessary. | 21<br>154<br>× 4<br>—<br>16 | 2<br>1,214<br>× 7<br>—<br>98 |
| **Step 3**<br>Multiply the hundreds.<br>Add any extra hundreds. | 21<br>154<br>× 4<br>—<br>616 | 1 2<br>1,214<br>× 7<br>—<br>498 |
| **Step 4**<br>Multiply the thousands.<br>Add any extra thousands. |  | 1 2<br>1,214<br>× 7<br>—<br>8,498 |

Find each product. Estimate to check reasonableness.

1.    185
   ×   4

2.    517
   ×   4

3.    2,741
   ×      3

4.    413
   ×   6

5.    2,625
   ×      6

6.    812
   ×   5

7.    3,711
   ×      8

8.    1,381
   ×      5

9. Molly and her sister each have 118 shells. How many shells do they have all together?

_____

10. A factory can make 2,418 footballs in 1 week. How many can it make in 9 weeks?

_____

Name _____

# Multiplying 3- and 4-Digit by 1-Digit Numbers

Find each product. Estimate to check reasonableness.

1.  352
    $\times$ 3

2.  2,768
    $\times$ 7

3.  482
    $\times$ 8

4.  3,521
    $\times$ 4

5.  4,219
    $\times$ 6

6.  385
    $\times$ 4

7.  632
    $\times$ 5

8.  1,848
    $\times$ 9

9. $7 \times 2,117 =$ _____

10. $6 \times 517 =$ _____

For **11** and **12**, use the table at the right.

11. If Player A scores the same number of runs each season, how many runs will he score in 5 seasons?

_____

12. If Player C scores the same number of runs each season, how many runs will he score in 8 seasons?

_____

**Runs Scored in 2010**

| Player | Runs Scored |
|--------|-------------|
| A      | 128         |
| B      | 113         |
| C      | 142         |

13. How many bottles of water would Tim sell if he sold 1,734 bottles each week for 4 weeks?

   **A** 5,886        **B** 6,836        **C** 6,928        **D** 6,936

14. If you know that $8 \times 300 = 2,400$, how can you find $8 \times 320$? Explain.

_____

_____

_____

# Using Rounding to Estimate

Use rounding to estimate 28 × 36.

| **Step 1** | **Step 2** |
|---|---|
| Round each number to the nearest 10. | Multiply 30 × 40. |

**Step 1**
Round each number to the nearest 10.

- Look at the digit in the ones place. Since it is greater than 5, add 1 to the digit in the rounding place.

- Change the digit to the right of the rounding place to 0.

28 rounds to 30 and 36 rounds to 40.

$$28 \times 36$$
$$\downarrow \quad \downarrow$$
$$30 \times 40$$

**Step 2**
Multiply 30 × 40.

30 × 40 = 1,200

So, 28 × 36 is about 1,200.

Use rounding to estimate each product.

**1.** 31 × 12

31 rounds to _____.

12 rounds to _____.

_____ × _____ = _____

**2.** 28 × 17

28 rounds to _____.

17 rounds to _____.

_____ × _____ = _____

**3.** 46 × 13 = _____

**4.** 52 × 42 = _____

**5.** 42 × 18 = _____

**6.** 38 × 36 = _____

**7.** 48 × 59 = _____

**8.** 71 × 34 = _____

**9.** 62 × 82 = _____

**10.** 95 × 21 = _____

**11.** The school store has 25 packages of erasers. There are 12 erasers in each package. About how many erasers does the school store have for sale?

_____

**12.** Chris estimated the product of 37 and 86 by multiplying 40 × 90. Tell how you know if this is greater than or less than the actual product.

_____

_____

# Using Rounding to Estimate

Use rounding to estimate each product.

**1.** 38 × 13 = _____    **2.** 41 × 18 = _____    **3.** 54 × 14 = _____

**4.** 44 × 22 = _____    **5.** 45 × 19 = _____    **6.** 34 × 48 = _____

**7.** 39 × 37 = _____    **8.** 25 × 81 = _____    **9.** 51 × 39 = _____

**10.** 48 × 29 = _____    **11.** 71 × 63 = _____    **12.** 82 × 54 = _____

**13.** A deep-sea fisherman went fishing 14 times last month. He caught 28 fish each time. About how many fish did he catch all together last month?

_____

**14.** Alligators lay between 20 and 50 eggs in a nest. A park ranger in Everglades National Park counted the number of eggs in 28 nests. On average, there were 40 eggs in each nest. About how many eggs did he count?

**A** 80          **C** 800

**B** 120         **D** 1,200

**15. Writing to Explain** Eric estimated 28 × 48 by finding 30 × 50. His estimate was 1,500, but he says the actual product will be greater than that amount. Is he correct? Explain how you know.

_____

_____

# Using Compatible Numbers to Estimate

Use compatible numbers to estimate 24 × 36.

Remember, compatible numbers are numbers that are easy to multiply.

**Step 1**
Pick compatible numbers.

• 24 is close to 25.

• 36 is close to 40.

24 × 36
↓  ↓
25 × 40

**Step 2**
Multiply the compatible numbers.

25 × 40 = 1,000

So, 24 × 36 is about 1,000.

Estimate to find each product.

1. $\_ × 12$

   $\_$ is close to 25.

   $\_$ is close to _____.

   $\_ ×$ _____ = _____

2. 24 × 31

   24 is close to 25.

   31 is close to _____.

   _____ × _____ = _____

3. $\_ × 26$

   $\_$ is close to _____.

   $\_$ is close to _____.

   ____ × _____ = _____

4. 63 × 59

   63 is close to _____.

   59 is close to _____.

   _____ × _____ = _____

5. $\_ × 24 =$ _____

6. 51 × 17 = _____

7. 82 × 78 = _____

8. $\_ × 61 =$ _____

9. 48 × 29 = _____

10. 53 × 39 = _____

11. There are 27 offices on each floor of a skyscraper. About how many offices are on 32 floors?

12. Yoko estimates that the product of 48 and 53 is 250. Is that reasonable? Why or why not?

# Using Compatible Numbers to Estimate

Estimate to find each product.

**1.** 27 × 39 = _____    **2.** 27 × 22 = _____    **3.** 24 × 34 = _____

**4.** 78 × 21 = _____    **5.** 41 × 48 = _____    **6.** 23 × 28 = _____

**7.** 44 × 44 = _____    **8.** 72 × 38 = _____    **9.** 52 × 42 = _____

**10.** 67 × 18 = _____    **11.** 46 × 19 = _____    **12.** 34 × 48 = _____

**13. Number Sense** Marc estimates 67 × 36 by finding 70 × 40. Will his estimate be greater or less than the actual product? Explain how you know.

_____

_____

**14.** A total of 42 people can ride a Ferris wheel at one time. What is the best way to estimate the number of people that ride the Ferris wheel in 26 rides?

A  40 × 20          C  40 × 25

B  30 × 30          D  40 × 50

**15. Writing to Explain** Describe how you can use compatible numbers to estimate 17 × 27.

_____

_____

# Problem Solving:
# Multiple-Step Problems

Chad and Amy cut lawns in their neighborhood to make money.
They charge $20 per lawn. One weekend, Amy cut 4 lawns, and
Chad cut 3 lawns. How much money did they earn all together?

**Solution One**

*Hidden Question:* How many lawns did
they mow all together?

Chad cut 3 lawns, Amy cut 4 lawns.

$$3 + 4 = 7$$

They cut 7 lawns.

*Question in the Problem:* How much
money did they earn all together?

$$7 \text{ lawns} \times \$20 = \$140$$

Chad and Amy earned $140.

**Solution Two**

*Hidden Question 1:* How much money did
Chad get for cutting lawns?

$$3 \times \$20 = \$60$$

*Hidden Question 2:* How much money did
Amy get for cutting lawns?

$$4 \times \$20 = \$80$$

*Question in the Problem:* How much money
did they earn all together?

$$\$60 + \$80 = \$140$$

Chad and Amy earned $140.

---

Write and answer the hidden question or questions. Then solve
the problem. Write your answer in a complete sentence.

1. Keisha sold 8 ribbons and 6 pins
   at a craft fair. She sold the ribbons
   for $3 each and the pins for $2
   each. How much money did
   Keisha earn?

   _____

   _____

   _____

   _____

   _____

2. Ken uses 6 apples and 2 bananas
   to make a fruit salad. He puts twice
   as many oranges as bananas in the
   salad. How many pieces of fruit will
   Ken use to make 2 fruit salads?

   _____

   _____

   _____

   _____

   _____

R 7·5

# Problem Solving: Multiple-Step Problems

For Exercise **1**, write and answer the hidden
question or questions. Then solve the problem.
Write your answer in a complete sentence.
Use the table at the right.

| County Fair Admission | |
|---|---|
| Adults | $5 |
| Students | $3 |
| Children | $2 |

1. Mario and his family went to the county
   fair. They bought 2 adult passes and
   3 children's passes. What was the
   total cost for the family?

   _____

   _____

   _____

   _____

2. A bus has 12 rows with 1 seat in each row on one side and
   12 rows with 2 seats in each row on the other side. How
   many seats does the bus have in all?

   **A** 3        **B** 12        **C** 24        **D** 36

3. What hidden questions do you need to answer in Exercise **2**?

   _____

   _____

4. **Writing to Explain** Write a problem about going to the laundromat
   that has a hidden question. A single load of laundry costs $2 and a
   double load costs $4. Explain how you solved your problem.

   _____

   _____

   _____

# Arrays and Multiplying 2-Digit Numbers

One way to find the product of 12 × 24 is by using an array.

Draw a rectangle 24 units long by 12 units wide.

Divide the rectangle by tens and ones for each factor.
Find the number of squares in each smaller rectangle. Then
add the numbers of squares in the four small rectangles.

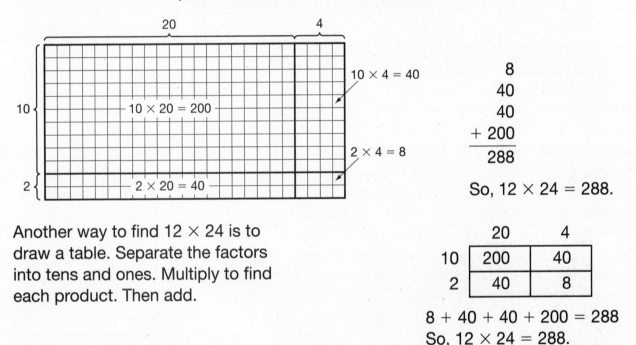

$$
\begin{array}{r}
8 \\
40 \\
40 \\
+ \ 200 \\
\hline
288
\end{array}
$$

So, 12 × 24 = 288.

Another way to find 12 × 24 is to
draw a table. Separate the factors
into tens and ones. Multiply to find
each product. Then add.

|     | 20  | 4   |
| --- | --- | --- |
| 10  | 200 | 40  |
| 2   | 40  | 8   |

8 + 40 + 40 + 200 = 288
So, 12 × 24 = 288.

---

Use the grid or table to find each product.

**1.** 11 × 22

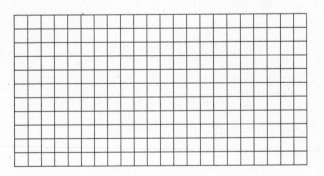

_____

**2.** 34 × 29

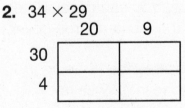

_____

Name _____

# Arrays and Multiplying 2-Digit Numbers

Use the grid to find each product.

**1.** 17 × 23

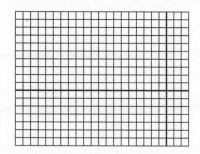

_____

**2.** 14 × 12

_____

Complete the table. Then find each product.

**3.** 31 × 19

**4.** 26 × 22

**5.** 33 × 14

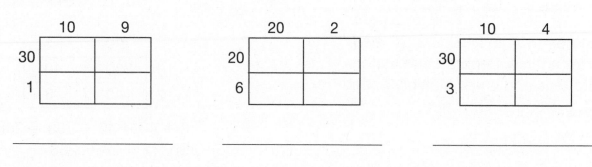

_____     _____     _____

**6.** 24 × 57 = _____          **7.** 44 × 48 = _____

**8.** A red kangaroo can cover 40 feet in 1 jump. How many feet can the red kangaroo cover in 12 jumps?                    _____

**9.** Barb exercises for 14 hours in 1 week. How many hours does she exercise in 32 weeks?

   **A** 496 hours     **B** 448 hours     **C** 420 hours     **D** 324 hours

**10. Writing to Explain** How is breaking apart the problem 16 × 34 like solving four simpler problems?

_____

Name _____

# Arrays and an Expanded Algorithm

You can use a place-value chart to organize the expanded algorithm to multiply.

Find $13 \times 82$.

| Multiply the ones. | | | | Multiply the tens. | | | | Add the partial products. | | | |
|---|---|---|---|---|---|---|---|---|---|---|---|
| Th | H | T | O | Th | H | T | O | Th | H | T | O |
| | | 8 | 2 | | | 8 | 2 | | | 8 | 2 |
| | × | 1 | 3 | | × | 1 | 3 | | × | 1 | 3 |
| | | | **6** | | | | 6 | | | | 6 |
| | **2** | **4** | **0** | | 2 | 4 | 0 | | 2 | 4 | 0 |
| | | | | | | **2** | **0** | | | 2 | 0 |
| | | | | | **8** | **0** | **0** | + | 8 | 0 | 0 |
| | | | | | | | | **1** | **0** | **6** | **6** |

So, $13 \times 82 = 1,066$.

Solve.

1. A large assortment box has 64 crayons in it. The art teacher buys 24 large assortment boxes of crayons at the start of the school year. How many crayons is this in all?

   _____

2. A new building will have 64 two-bedroom apartments. Each apartment will need 18 electrical outlets. How many outlets will the electricians have to install in all 64 apartments?

   _____

3. **Number Sense** Use the place-value chart at the right to multiply $45 \times 37$. Be sure to record each partial product in the correct column of the chart. Beside each partial product, record the numbers you multiplied. Then find the final product.

| Th | H | T | O | |
|---|---|---|---|---|
| | | 3 | 7 | What I |
| | × | 4 | 5 | Multiply |
| | | | | |
| | | | | _____ |
| | | | | _____ |
| + | | | | _____ |
| | | | | _____ |

# Arrays and an Expanded Algorithm

Find each partial product. Then add to find the product.

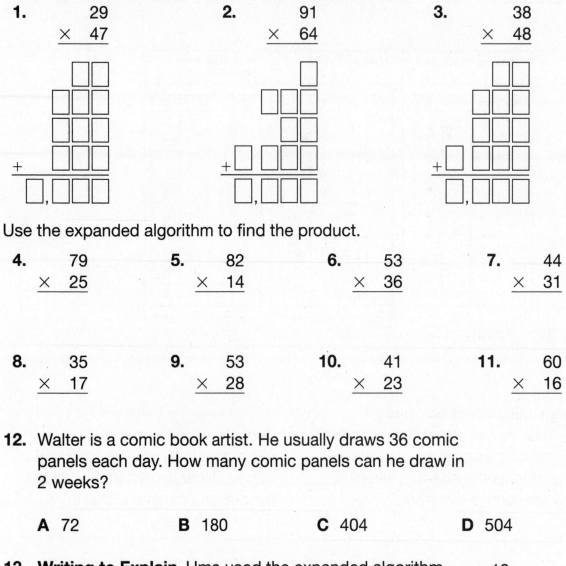

**1.**  29
   ×  47

**2.**  91
   ×  64

**3.**  38
   ×  48

Use the expanded algorithm to find the product.

**4.**  79
   ×  25

**5.**  82
   ×  14

**6.**  53
   ×  36

**7.**  44
   ×  31

**8.**  35
   ×  17

**9.**  53
   ×  28

**10.**  41
    ×  23

**11.**  60
    ×  16

**12.** Walter is a comic book artist. He usually draws 36 comic panels each day. How many comic panels can he draw in 2 weeks?

**A** 72          **B** 180          **C** 404          **D** 504

**13. Writing to Explain** Uma used the expanded algorithm to solve 62 × 13. Her work is shown at the right. What did she do wrong? Explain what partial products Uma should have added to find the correct product.

```
    13
×   62
     6
     2
   180
+   60
   248
```

Name _____

# Using Compatible Numbers to Estimate

Use compatible numbers to estimate 24 × 36.

Remember, compatible numbers are numbers that are easy to multiply.

**Step 1**
Pick compatible numbers.

- 24 is close to 25.

- 36 is close to 40.

24 × 36
↓ ↓
25 × 40

**Step 2**
Multiply the compatible numbers.

25 × 40 = 1,000

So, 24 × 36 is about 1,000.

Estimate to find each product.

**1.** 23 × 12
23 is close to 25.

12 is close to _____.

25 × _____ = _____

**2.** 24 × 31
24 is close to 25.

31 is close to _____.

_____ × _____ = _____

**3.** 42 × 26
42 is close to_____.

26 is close to _____.

_____ × _____ = _____

**4.** 63 × 59
63 is close to_____.

59 is close to _____.

_____ × _____ = _____

**5.** 19 × 24 = _____

**6.** 51 × 17 = _____

**7.** 82 × 78 = _____

**8.** 24 × 61 = _____

**9.** 48 × 29 = _____

**10.** 53 × 39 = _____

**11.** There are 27 offices on each floor of a skyscraper. About how many offices are on 32 floors?

**12.** Yoko estimates that the product of 48 and 53 is 250. Is that reasonable? Why or why not?

_____

_____

# Using Compatible Numbers to Estimate

Estimate to find each product.

**1.** 27 × 39 = _____  **2.** 27 × 22 = _____  **3.** 24 × 34 = _____

**4.** 78 × 21 = _____  **5.** 41 × 48 = _____  **6.** 23 × 28 = _____

**7.** 44 × 44 = _____  **8.** 72 × 38 = _____  **9.** 52 × 42 = _____

**10.** 67 × 18 = _____  **11.** 46 × 19 = _____  **12.** 34 × 48 = _____

**13. Number Sense** Marc estimates 67 × 36 by finding 70 × 40.
Will his estimate be greater or less than the actual product?
Explain how you know.

_____

_____

**14.** A total of 42 people can ride a Ferris wheel at one time.
What is the best way to estimate the number of people
that ride the Ferris wheel in 26 rides?

    **A** 40 × 20    **C** 40 × 25

    **B** 30 × 30    **D** 40 × 50

**15. Writing to Explain** Describe how you can use compatible numbers to
estimate 17 × 27.

_____

_____

# Multiplying 2-Digit Numbers by Multiples of 10

Find the product of 60 and 26.

One way to find 60 × 26 is to use a grid.
Show 60 rows with 26 squares in each row.

Break apart 26 into tens and ones: 26 = 20 + 6.

Draw a vertical line on the grid to separate the
grid into two sections. Label one section 60 × 20.
Label the other section 60 × 6.

Multiply to find the partial products:
60 × 20 = 1,200 and 60 × 6 = 360.

Add the partial products:
1,200 + 360 = 1,560. So, 60 × 26 = 1,560.

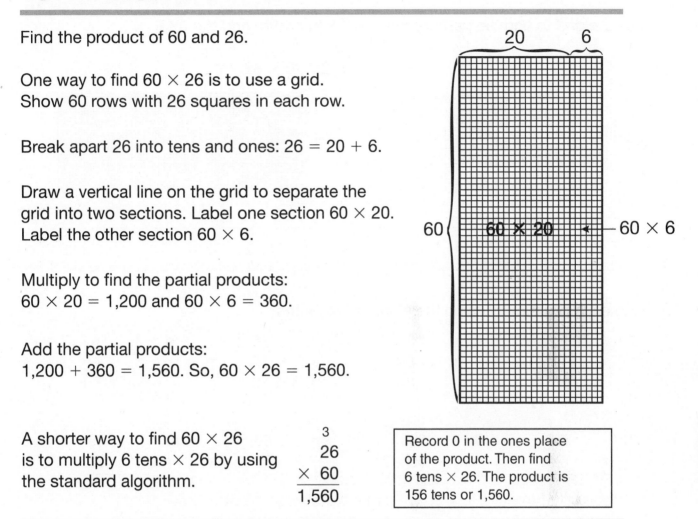

A shorter way to find 60 × 26
is to multiply 6 tens × 26 by using
the standard algorithm.

$$\begin{array}{r} 3 \\ 26 \\ \times\ 60 \\ \hline 1{,}560 \end{array}$$

Record 0 in the ones place
of the product. Then find
6 tens × 26. The product is
156 tens or 1,560.

For Exercises **1** through **5**, find each product.

**1.** 23 × 40 _____

**2.** 16 × 30 _____

**3.** 34 × 50 _____

**4.** 60 × 47 _____

**5.** 17 × 80 _____

# Multiplying 2-Digit Numbers by Multiples of 10

Use the grid to find the partial products. Then add to find the total.

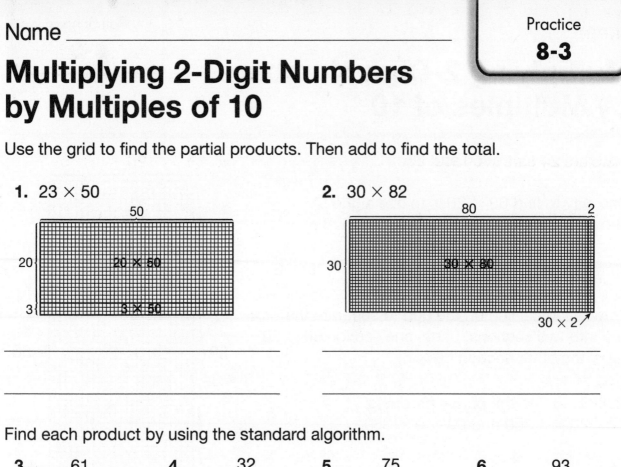

**1.** 23 × 50

50

20    20 × 50

3    3 × 50

_____

_____

**2.** 30 × 82

80        2

30    30 × 80

30 × 2

_____

_____

Find each product by using the standard algorithm.

| **3.** | 61 | **4.** | 32 | **5.** | 75 | **6.** | 93 |
|---|---|---|---|---|---|---|---|
| | × 30 | | × 60 | | × 70 | | × 50 |
| | ☐☐30 | | ☐☐20 | | ☐☐☐0 | | 4☐☐☐ |

| **7.** | 66 | **8.** | 53 | **9.** | 86 | **10.** | 39 |
|---|---|---|---|---|---|---|---|
| | × 20 | | × 40 | | × 80 | | × 90 |

**11.** Which numbers are the partial products of 77 × 30?

    **A** 210 and 700         **B** 2,100 and 210

    **C** 511 and 2,100       **D** 4,900 and 210

**12. Writing to Explain** Explain how you can solve 40 × 16 by breaking apart the numbers.

_____

_____

# Multiplying 2-Digit by 2-Digit Numbers

There are 24 cars in a race. Each car has 13 workers in the pit area. How many pit-area workers are at the race in all?

| **Step 1** | **Step 2** | **Step 3** |
|---|---|---|
| Multiply the ones. | Multiply the tens. | Add the partial products. |
| Regroup if necessary. | Regroup if necessary. | |

**Step 1**

Multiply the ones.
Regroup if necessary.

$$\begin{array}{r} 1 \\ 24 \\ \times\ 13 \\ \hline 72 \end{array} \leftarrow 3 \times 24$$

**Step 2**

Multiply the tens.
Regroup if necessary.

$$\begin{array}{r} 24 \\ \times\ 13 \\ \hline 72 \\ 240 \end{array} \leftarrow 10 \times 24$$

**Step 3**

Add the partial products.

$$\begin{array}{r} 24 \\ \times\ 13 \\ \hline 72 \\ +\ 240 \\ \hline 312 \end{array}$$

$24 \times 13 = 312$, so there are 312 pit-area workers at the race.

---

Find each product. Start multiplying the ones. Then multiply the tens.

1.  $\begin{array}{r} 38 \\ \times\ 26 \\ \hline \end{array}$

2.  $\begin{array}{r} 67 \\ \times\ 27 \\ \hline \end{array}$

3.  $\begin{array}{r} 47 \\ \times\ 85 \\ \hline \end{array}$

4.  $\begin{array}{r} 88 \\ \times\ 32 \\ \hline \end{array}$

5.  $\begin{array}{r} 53 \\ \times\ 48 \\ \hline \end{array}$

6.  $\begin{array}{r} 18 \\ \times\ 77 \\ \hline \end{array}$

7.  $\begin{array}{r} 67 \\ \times\ 34 \\ \hline \end{array}$

8.  $\begin{array}{r} 91 \\ \times\ 46 \\ \hline \end{array}$

9.  **Reasonableness** Corina multiplied $62 \times 22$ and found a product of 1,042. Explain why Corina's answer is not reasonable.

_____

_____

_____

_____

Name _____

# Multiplying 2-Digit by 2-Digit Numbers

Find the product.

1.  54
   × 17
   _____

2.  36
   × 20
   _____

3.  53
   × 12
   _____

4.  48
   × 46
   _____

5.  37
   × 83
   _____

6.  62
   × 17
   _____

7.  91
   × 49
   _____

8.  28
   × 56
   _____

9.  70
   × 39
   _____

10.  58
    × 90
    _____

11.  97
    × 42
    _____

12.  64
    × 88
    _____

13. A carton holds 24 bottles of juice. How many juice bottles are in 15 cartons?

_____

14. How much do 21 bushels of sweet corn weigh?

_____

15. How much do 18 bushels of asparagus weigh?

_____

| Vegetable | Weight of 1 Bushel |
|-----------|--------------------|
| Asparagus | 24 pounds |
| Beets | 52 pounds |
| Carrots | 50 pounds |
| Sweet corn | 35 pounds |

16. How much more do 13 bushels of beets weigh than 13 bushels of carrots?      _____

17. Which of the following is a reasonable answer for 92 × 98?

   **A** 1,800      **B** 9,000      **C** 18,000      **D** 90,000

18. **Writing to Explain** Garth is multiplying 29 × 16. He found the partial product 174 after multiplying the ones and 290 after multiplying the tens. Explain how Garth can find the final product.

_____

# Problem Solving:
# Two-Question Problems

**Read and Understand**

**Problem 1:** Gina gave 3 sheets of paper to each of the 12 students in her class. How many sheets of paper did she give out?

**Problem 2:** Each sheet of paper had 3 paper clips attached to it. How many paper clips did she give out?

Answer Problem 1 first.

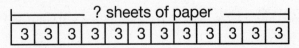

12 students × 3 sheets of paper = 36 sheets of paper
Gina gave out 36 sheets of paper.

**Plan and Solve**

Use the answer from Problem 1 to solve Problem 2.

36 sheets of paper × 3 paper clips = 108 paper clips
Gina gave out 108 paper clips.

---

Solve. Use the answer from Problem 1 to solve Problem 2.

1. **Problem 1:** April made 16 baskets and glued 5 flowers on each one. How many flowers did she use in all?

   **Problem 2:** Each flower April used had 8 petals. How many petals were there on all the flowers she used?

   _____

2. **Problem 1:** Jorge washed cars for four hours on Saturday. In the first hour, he washed 4 cars. In the second hour, he washed 7 cars. In the third hour, he washed 9 cars. How many cars did he wash in the first three hours?

   **Problem 2:** Jorge washed the same number of cars in the fourth hour as he did in the first three hours combined. How many cars did he wash in all in four hours?

Name _____

# Problem Solving:
# Two-Question Problems

For **1** and **2**, use the answer from the first problem to solve the second problem.

1. **Problem 1:** Francisco reads 75 pages every week for a summer reading program. If there are about 4 weeks in a month, then how many pages can Francisco read in a month?

_____

**Problem 2:** How many pages will Francisco read in the 3 months of summer?

_____

2. **Problem 1:** Mr. Dunn drives a 12-mile round trip 3 times a week to the dog park. How many miles does he drive?

_____

**Problem 2:** Mr. Dunn estimates he uses 4 gallons of gas over the course of the week to and from the dog park. How many miles per gallon does his car get?

_____

3. **Problem 1:** A company buys printer paper in a box that contains 8 packages. Which expression shows how many packages of paper are in 12 boxes?

   **A** $8 + 8$       **B** $8 \div 2$       **C** $8 + 12$       **D** $8 \times 12$

**Problem 2:** Each package of paper costs 3 dollars. Explain how to find how much 12 boxes of printer paper will cost.

_____

_____

_____

# Using Mental Math to Divide

When dividing numbers that end in zero, you can use basic division facts, as well as patterns, to help you divide mentally. For example:

| | Find 210 ÷ 7. | Find 4,200 ÷ 6. |
|---|---|---|
| What You **Think** | First, find the basic fact.<br>**210 ÷ 7 =**<br>**21 ÷ 7 =**<br>**21** tens **÷ 7 =**<br>3 tens or 30 | Find the basic fact.<br>**4,200 ÷ 6 =**<br>**42 ÷ 6 =**<br>**42** hundreds **÷ 6 =**<br>7 hundreds or 700 |
| What You **Write** | 210 ÷ 7 = 30 | 4,200 ÷ 6 = 700 |

Divide. Use mental math.

1. 250 ÷ 5 = _____

2. 7,200 ÷ 9 = _____

3. 200 ÷ 4 = _____

4. 2,800 ÷ 7 = _____

5. 810 ÷ 9 = _____

6. 5,000 ÷ 5 = _____

7. **Number Sense** What basic fact would you use to help solve 4,500 ÷ 9? _____

8. In 1 week there are 7 days. How many weeks are in 210 days? _____

9. How many weeks are there in 420 days? _____

# Using Mental Math to Divide

Divide. Use mental math.

1. 250 ÷ 5 = _____

2. 1,400 ÷ 2 = _____

3. 300 ÷ 5 = _____

4. 1,600 ÷ 4 = _____

5. 240 ÷ 8 = _____

6. 3,600 ÷ 4 = _____

7. 1,600 ÷ 2 = _____

8. 270 ÷ 3 = _____

9. 4,200 ÷ 7 = _____

10. 640 ÷ 8 = _____

11. 2,000 ÷ 5 = _____

12. 320 ÷ 8 = _____

13. 1,200 ÷ 2 = _____

14. 1,600 ÷ 8 = _____

The fourth grade performed a play based on the story of Cinderella. There was one chair for each person present.

15. On Friday, 140 people came to the play. The chairs in the auditorium were arranged in 7 equal rows. How many chairs were in each row? _____

16. There were 8 equal rows set up for Saturday's performance. There were 240 people at the play on Saturday. How many chairs were in each row? _____

17. Which is the quotient of 5,600 ÷ 8?

A 40            B 400            C 70            D 700

18. **Writing to Explain** Explain why the following answer is not correct: 1,000 ÷ 5 = 2,000.

_____

_____

_____

# Estimating Quotients

**Estimate** 460 ÷ 9.

You can use compatible numbers.

Ask yourself: What is a number close to 460 that could be easily divided by 9? Try 450.

$450 \div 9 = 50$

So, 460 ÷ 9 is about 50.

50 is a good estimation for this problem.

You can also estimate by thinking about multiplication.

Ask yourself: Nine times what number is about 460?

$9 \times 5 = 45$, so $9 \times 50 = 450$.

So, 460 ÷ 9 is about 50.

Estimate each quotient.

**1.** 165 ÷ 4 _____

**2.** 35 ÷ 4 _____

**3.** 715 ÷ 9 _____

**4.** 490 ÷ 8 _____

**5.** 512 ÷ 5 _____

**6.** 652 ÷ 8 _____

**7.** 790 ÷ 9 _____

**8.** 200 ÷ 7 _____

**9.** 311 ÷ 6 _____

**10. Number Sense** Complete by filling in the circle with < or >. Without dividing, explain how you know which quotient is greater.
315 ÷ 5 ◯ 347 ÷ 5

_____

_____

Name _____

# Estimating Quotients

Estimate each quotient.

**1.** 82 ÷ 4        _____

**2.** 580 ÷ 3       _____

**3.** 96 ÷ 5        _____

**4.** 811 ÷ 2       _____

**5.** 194 ÷ 6       _____

**6.** 207 ÷ 7       _____

**7.** 282 ÷ 4       _____

**8.** 479 ÷ 8       _____

**9.** Jacqui is writing a book. If she needs to
write 87 pages in 9 days, about how
many pages will she write each day?        _____

**10.** Wade wants to give 412 of his marbles to
10 of his friends. If he gives each friend
the same number of marbles, about
how many will each friend receive?        _____

**11.** Which is the best estimate for 502 ÷ 6?

   **A** 60        **B** 70        **C** 80        **D** 90

**12.** **Writing to Explain** You are using division to determine
how much whole wheat flour to use in a bread recipe. Is an
estimated answer good enough?

_____

_____

# Estimating Quotients for Greater Dividends

Find 294 ÷ 5.

Think of multiples of 5.    5, 10, 15, 20, 25, 30

Underline the first two digits of <u>29</u>4.

Find the multiple of 5 that is closest to 29. That multiple is 30.

$6 \times 5 = 30$, so
$60 \times 5 = 300$.
$300 \div 5 = 60$

294 ÷ 5 is about 60.

Estimate each quotient.

**1.** 1,561 ÷ 8

Think of multiples of 8.   8, 16, _____, _____, 40, _____

Underline the first two digits of 1,561.

Which multiple of 8 is closest to 15? _____

What is 200 × 8? _____

What is 1,600 ÷ 8? _____

So, 1,561 ÷ 8 is about _____.

**2.** 461 ÷ 9 _____

**3.** 2,356 ÷ 6 _____

**4.** 5,352 ÷ 9 _____

Name _____

# Estimating Quotients for Greater Dividends

Estimate each quotient.

**1.** 381 ÷ 5 _____

**2.** 5,985 ÷ 9 _____

**3.** 2,753 ÷ 7 _____

**4.** 190 ÷ 8 _____

**5.** 427 ÷ 6 _____

**6.** 1,127 ÷ 4 _____

**7.** 143 ÷ 3 _____

**8.** 386 ÷ 9 _____

**9.** 4,088 ÷ 5 _____

**10.** 1,378 ÷ 4 _____

**11.** 4,405 ÷ 6 _____

**12.** 812 ÷ 7 _____

**13.** 3,942 ÷ 8 _____

**14.** 933 ÷ 3 _____

**15.** 4,471 ÷ 7 _____

**16.** 5,251 ÷ 9 _____

**17.** Daniel's family grows pecans. Last year they harvested 1,309 pounds of pecans. If they packed bags with 3 pounds of pecans in each bag, about how many bags would they fill?

**A** 40 bags  **B** 50 bags  **C** 400 bags  **D** 500 bags

**18. Reason** At Camp Summer Fun, 4 campers share each tent. The camp is expecting 331 campers. About how many tents will they need? Will the number of tents they actually need be more or less than the estimate? How do you know?

_____

_____

Name _____

# Dividing with Remainders

When you divide, you can think of putting items into groups.
For example:

$$60 \div 6 = 10$$

60 items    6 groups    10 items in each group

Sometimes there are items left over. In division, the number of
"left over" items is called the **remainder**. For example:

$$62 \div 6 = 10 \text{ R2} \longrightarrow \text{2 items left over}$$

62 items    6 groups    10 items in each group

Divide. You may use counters or pictures to help.

**1.** $4\overline{)34}$      **2.** $8\overline{)65}$      **3.** $9\overline{)75}$

**4.** $6\overline{)27}$      **5.** $5\overline{)14}$      **6.** $9\overline{)37}$

**7. Number Sense** In division, why should the remainder not
be greater than the divisor?

_____

Name _____

# Dividing with Remainders

Divide. You may use counters or pictures to help.

**1.** 4)27          **2.** 6)32          **3.** 7)17          **4.** 9)29

**5.** 8)27          **6.** 3)27          **7.** 5)28          **8.** 4)35

**9.** 2)19          **10.** 7)30         **11.** 3)17         **12.** 9)16

If you arrange these items into equal rows, tell how many will be in each row and how many will be left over.

**13.** 26 shells into 3 rows          _____

**14.** 19 pennies into 5 rows         _____

**15.** 17 balloons into 7 rows        _____

**16.** **Reasonableness** Ms. Nikkel wants to divide her class of 23 students into 4 equal teams. Is this reasonable? Why or why not?

_____

_____

**17.** Which is the remainder for the quotient of 79 ÷ 8?

   **A** 7          **B** 6          **C** 5          **D** 4

**18.** **Writing to Explain** Pencils are sold in packages of 5. Explain why you need 6 packages in order to have enough for 27 students.

_____

_____

# Multiplication and Division Stories

Multiply when you want to combine equal groups, and divide when you want to find the number of groups. You can draw a picture to help you interpret a story and turn it into a math problem.

A bicycle wheel has 36 spokes and spokes are sold in packages of 5. How many packages must you buy to replace all the spokes in a wheel?

**You can draw a picture that shows the spokes in a package.**

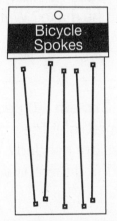

1. Do you want to combine equal groups or do you want to find the number of groups?

_____

2. Do you want to multiply or divide? _____

3. What is the number expression for this problem? _____

4. What is the solution to the expression? _____

5. How many packages must you buy? _____

6. **Writing to Explain** Why are the previous two answers different from each other?

_____

_____

Name _____

# Multiplication and Division Stories

Use the story to solve questions **1** through **4**.

1. 3 litters were born at Broadway Kennel last year, and each litter had 7 puppies. How many puppies were born at Broadway Kennel last year?

   _____

2. **Geometry** Martin is making squares by arranging 26 sticks. How many squares can he make? Write and solve the number fact you used to find the answer.

   _____

3. **Writing to Explain** 60 people will be attending a dinner party. Each table at the party can seat 8 people. How many tables are needed? Write and solve the number fact you used to find the answer, and explain your reasoning.

   _____

   _____

   _____

   _____

4. In a parking lot, some cars have 1 spare tire and others have no spare tires. All together, there are 43 tires and 9 cars. How many cars have a spare tire?

   _____

   _____

Write a multiplication story using the multiplication problem below. Then solve.

5. 14 × 4

   _____

   _____

   _____

# Using Objects to Divide: Division as Repeated Subtraction

When you divide, you subtract equal groups.

Doris has 32 strawberries. She makes box lunches by putting 4 strawberries in each box lunch. How many box lunches can she make this way?

**What you think:** Doris will put 4 strawberries in each lunch box. How many lunch boxes can she make?

**What you show:** Repeated subtraction

| | |
|---|---|
| $32 - 4 = 28$ | $16 - 4 = 12$ |
| $28 - 4 = 24$ | $12 - 4 = 8$ |
| $24 - 4 = 20$ | $8 - 4 = 4$ |
| $20 - 4 = 16$ | $4 - 4 = 0$ |

You can subtract 4 from 32 eight times.

**What you write:** $32 \div 4 = 8$

32 is the dividend, the number that is being divided.

4 is the divisor, the number the dividend is being divided by.

8 is the quotient, or the answer to the division problem.

Draw pictures to solve each problem.

1. You have 15 marbles. You put 5 marbles into each group. How many groups can you make?

   _____

2. You have 20 ice cubes. You put 4 ice cubes into each glass. How many glasses can you put ice cubes into?

   _____

# Using Objects to Divide: Division as Repeated Subtraction

Draw pictures to solve each problem.

1. Anthony has 18 stickers. He wants to give 3 stickers to each of his friends. How many friends can he give stickers to?

   _____

2. Mrs. Riggins has 40 glass tiles. She is going to put 8 glass tiles on each clay pot she is decorating. How many clay pots can she decorate this way?

   _____

3. There are 21 students in Mr. Tentler's class. The class is being separated into groups of 3 students. How many groups can they form?

   _____

4. Ca___ reads a book that has 90 pages. If he reads 10 pages eac___ ay, how many days will it take him to finish reading the ___ ?

   **A** 3 ___

   **B** 6 da___

   **C** 9 day___

   **D** 12 days

5. A school distric___ ___ flags to give to schools. If it gives 4 flags to each sc___ ___ow many schools can it give flags to? Explain your ans___

   _____

   _____

# Division as Repeated Subtraction

For City Clean-Up Day, 18 people volunteered to clean up the city park. The volunteers worked in groups with 3 people each. How many groups of volunteers cleaned up the city park?

Use repeated subtraction to find the number of groups.

$18 - 3 = 15$
$15 - 3 = 12$
$12 - 3 = 9$
$9 - 3 = 6$
$6 - 3 = 3$
$3 - 3 = 0$

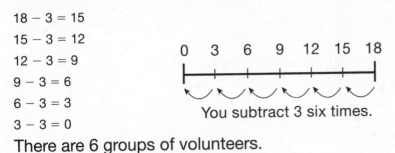

You subtract 3 six times.

There are 6 groups of volunteers.

Use repeated subtraction to divide. Use a number line to help.

0 1 2 3 4 5 6 7 8 9 10 11 12 13 14 15 16 17 18 19 20 21 22 23 24 25 26 27 28 29 30

1. Mark is placing 12 model cars into equal groups. Each group has 4 model cars. How many groups of model cars will he make?

_____

2. There are 24 students in gym class. They divided into teams of 6 for a volleyball game. How many teams were there?

_____

3. Each necklace Cara makes has 5 beads. How many necklaces can Cara make with 20 beads?

_____

4. Amy has 12 dolls in her collection. She places 6 dolls on each shelf. How many shelves does she need?

_____

5. Charlie has 16 chores to do. He can complete 4 chores in one day. How many days will Charlie take to complete his chores?

_____

6. The pet store has 9 parakeets. If 3 parakeets are in each cage, how many cages are there?

_____

7. Shawn needs to learn how to play 15 songs for his band's concert. If he learns 3 songs each week, how many weeks will it take him to learn all of the songs?

_____

8. At Rosa Elementary School, 27 teachers signed up to carpool. If 3 teachers ride together in each car, how many cars are needed for all of the teachers?

_____

Name _____

# Division as Repeated Subtraction

Use repeated subtraction to solve each problem. Draw pictures to help.

1. Roger buys a package of 16 rawhide bones for his dog. He gives his dog 4 bones each week. How many weeks will the package of rawhide bones last?

   _____

2. During recess 24 students divided into kickball teams. Each team had 6 players. How many teams were there?

   _____

3. Each member of a juggling troop juggles 6 balls at one time. The jugglers use 18 balls during a show. How many jugglers are in the show?

   _____

4. The county fair has 4 people working at the snack bar each shift. If 32 people work at the snack bar each day, how many shifts are there?

   _____

5. For a piano recital, Jessie is playing a song that is 3 minutes long. She practices by playing the song several times in a row. If she practices for 21 minutes, how many times does she play the song?

   **A** 6　　　　　　**B** 7　　　　　　**C** 8　　　　　　**D** 9

6. Ryan wants to prepare for a mini-marathon by jogging 12 miles each week. How many days would he need to jog if he runs only 3 miles each day? Explain.

   _____

   _____

# Using Objects to Divide: Division as Sharing

You can use models to help you solve division problems.
The models below help you find 78 ÷ 5.
Find 78 ÷ 5.
Estimate 80 ÷ 5 = 16.

First divide the tens.

Now, change the tens into the ones.

Now, divide the ones.

Now, write the remainder.

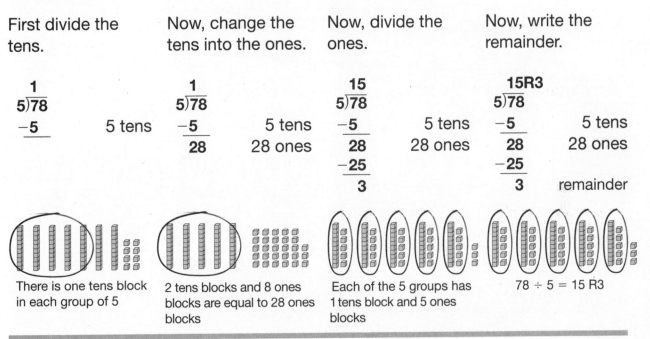

There is one tens block in each group of 5

2 tens blocks and 8 ones blocks are equal to 28 ones blocks

Each of the 5 groups has 1 tens block and 5 ones blocks

$78 ÷ 5 = 15$ R3

Use the models below to help you fill in the boxes.

**1.** 66 ÷ [  ] = [  ] R2

**2.** 97 ÷ 4 = [  ] R [  ]

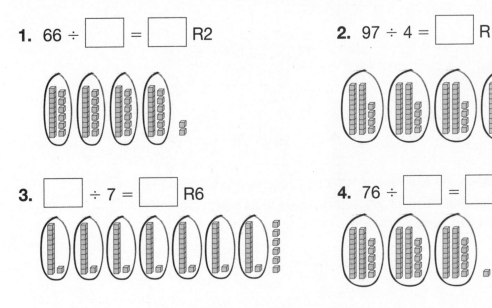

**3.** [  ] ÷ 7 = [  ] R6

**4.** 76 ÷ [  ] = [  ] R [  ]

Name _____

# Using Objects to Divide: Division as Sharing

Draw pictures to tell how many are in each group and how many are left over.

**1.** 57 CDs in 8 organizers

**2.** 62 stickers on 5 rolls

_____

**3.** 44 plants in 6 rows

**4.** 37 chairs for 9 tables

_____

In **5** through **8**, use the model to complete each division sentence.

**5.** 27 ÷ ☐ = ☐ R3

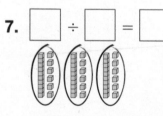

**6.** ☐ ÷ 9 = ☐

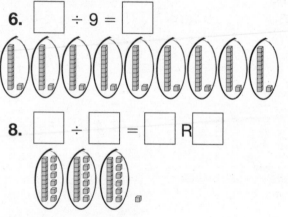

**7.** ☐ ÷ ☐ = ☐

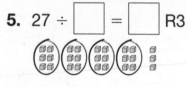

**8.** ☐ ÷ ☐ = ☐ R ☐

**9.** Ken has 72 marbles. He decides to share them with his friends so they can play a game. Which of the following models shows Ken sharing his marbles?

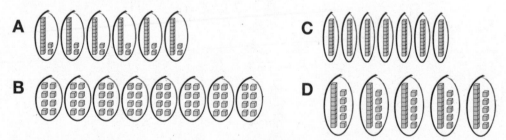

A

C

B

D

**10. Writing to Explain** At Mr. Horne's farm there are 53 cows. There are 4 people who milk the cows each day. Does each person milk the same number of cows? Use a model to help you.

_____

_____

# Dividing 2-Digit by 1-Digit Numbers

You can find 2-digit quotients by breaking apart the problem and dividing tens, then ones.

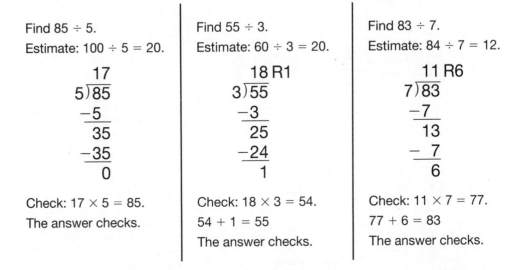

Find 85 ÷ 5.
Estimate: 100 ÷ 5 = 20.

$$
\begin{array}{r}
17 \\
5\overline{)85} \\
-5 \\
\hline
35 \\
-35 \\
\hline
0
\end{array}
$$

Check: 17 × 5 = 85.
The answer checks.

Find 55 ÷ 3.
Estimate: 60 ÷ 3 = 20.

$$
\begin{array}{r}
18\,R1 \\
3\overline{)55} \\
-3 \\
\hline
25 \\
-24 \\
\hline
1
\end{array}
$$

Check: 18 × 3 = 54.
54 + 1 = 55
The answer checks.

Find 83 ÷ 7.
Estimate: 84 ÷ 7 = 12.

$$
\begin{array}{r}
11\,R6 \\
7\overline{)83} \\
-7 \\
\hline
13 \\
-\;7 \\
\hline
6
\end{array}
$$

Check: 11 × 7 = 77.
77 + 6 = 83
The answer checks.

Find the missing values.

**1.**

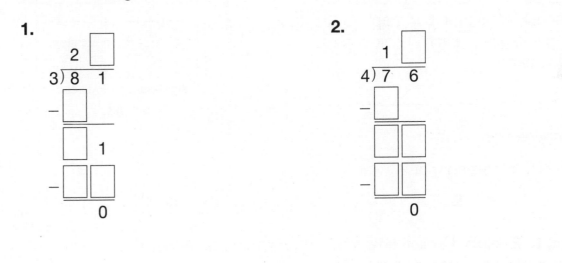

**2.**

**3.** 3)91

**4.** 4)86

**5.** 2)75

Name _____

# Dividing 2-Digit by 1-Digit Numbers

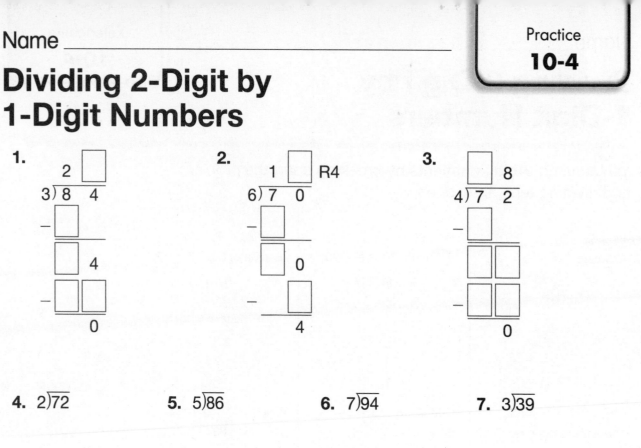

**1.**

```
     2 ☐
  3)8 4
  -☐
  ──
    ☐4
  -☐☐
  ──
     0
```

**2.**

```
     1 ☐ R4
  6)7 0
  -☐
  ──
    ☐0
  -☐
  ──
     4
```

**3.**

```
     ☐ 8
  4)7 2
  -☐
  ──
   ☐☐
  -☐☐
  ──
     0
```

**4.** 2)72     **5.** 5)86     **6.** 7)94     **7.** 3)39

**8.** 8)99     **9.** 5)87     **10.** 2)96     **11.** 3)43

Mrs. Thomas is planning to provide snacks for 96 fourth graders when they go on a field trip to the aquarium. Each student will receive 1 of each snack. Using the bar graph to the right, how many packages of each snack does Mrs. Thomas need?

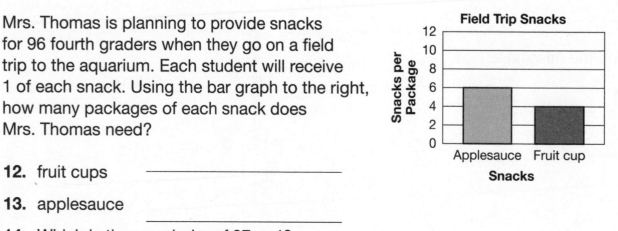

**Field Trip Snacks**

**12.** fruit cups     _____

**13.** applesauce     _____

**14.** Which is the remainder of 27 ÷ 4?

**A** 1          **B** 2          **C** 3          **D** 4

**15. Writing to Explain** Explain how to find the number of leftover pencils if Wendy wants to share 37 pencils with 9 people.

_____

_____

_____

# Dividing 3-Digit by 1-Digit Numbers

You can find 3-digit quotients by breaking apart the problem.

Find 528 ÷ 4.          Find 575 ÷ 5.          Find 725 ÷ 3.
Estimate 500 ÷ 4 = 125.   Estimate 600 ÷ 5 = 120.   Estimate 750 ÷ 3 = 250.

```
     132              115              241 R2
  4)528            5)575            3)725
   - 4              - 5              - 6
    12                7               12
   - 12             - 5              - 12
     8               25                5
   -  8            -  25             -  3
     0                0                2
```

Check 132 × 4 = 528   Check 115 × 5 = 575   Check 241 × 3 = 723
The answer checks.   The answer checks.   723 + 2 = 725
                                          The answer checks.

Find the missing values.

**1.**
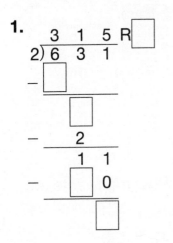

**2.**
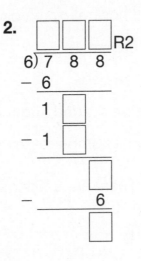

**3.** 3)462      **4.** 5)640      **5.** 9)919

Name _____

# Dividing 3-Digit by
# 1-Digit Numbers

In **1** through **8**, use place-value blocks to help you divide.

**1.** 4)412  **2.** 6)936  **3.** 7)798  **4.** 7)806

**5.** 3)420  **6.** 5)619  **7.** 7)842  **8.** 8)856

**9.** A train can hold 444 people in rows with 4 seats. How many 4-seat rows are there? _____

**10.** A song has 540 beats. If the song is 3 minutes long, how many beats per minute does the song have? _____

**11.** **Geometry** A circle has 360 degrees. If the circle is divided in half, how many degrees does each half measure? _____

**12.** Harvey has 513 stamps. He places an equal number in 3 stamp books. How many stamps are in each book? _____

**13.** Zeeshan has collected 812 autographs. Each autograph is either from a baseball star, a football star, a movie star, or a rock star. He has an equal number of autographs for each group. How many autographs does he have in each group? _____

**14.** Nicole has 369 tea bags. There are 3 different flavors of tea. What information do you need to find how many tea bags Nicole has of each flavor?

**A** The number of flavors

**B** The number of tea bags

**C** If a tea bag can be divided into fourths

**D** If there is an equal number of tea bags for each flavor

**15.** An ant has 6 legs. There are 870 legs in José's ant farm. How many ants are there in his ant farm?

**A** 14 R5  **B** 145  **C** 864  **D** 5,220

**16.** **Writing to Explain** Jeff has 242 DVDs. He has 2 shelves that can each hold 120 DVDs. Does he need to buy another shelf?

_____

# Deciding Where to Start Dividing

Sometimes there are not enough hundreds to divide by.
Sometimes you have to break up the hundreds into 10 tens.

Find 325 ÷ 5.
Estimate 300 ÷ 5 = 60.

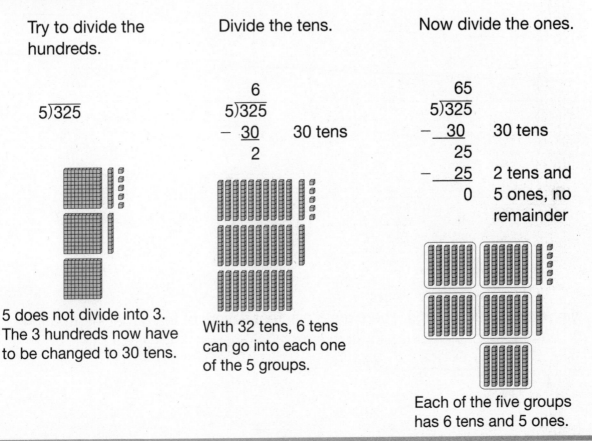

| Try to divide the hundreds. | Divide the tens. | Now divide the ones. |
|---|---|---|
| 5)‾325 | 6<br>5)‾325<br>− 30   30 tens<br>2 | 65<br>5)‾325<br>− 30   30 tens<br>25<br>− 25   2 tens and<br>0   5 ones, no remainder |
| 5 does not divide into 3. The 3 hundreds now have to be changed to 30 tens. | With 32 tens, 6 tens can go into each one of the 5 groups. | Each of the five groups has 6 tens and 5 ones. |

Find the missing values in the problems below.

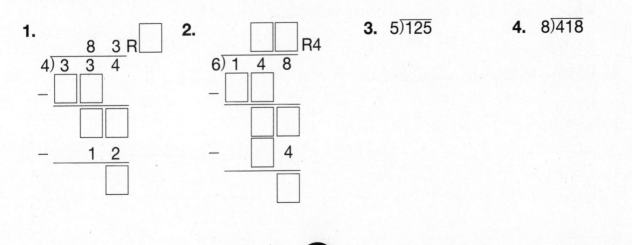

**1.**

```
      8  3 R□
  4)3 3 4
  −□□
    □□
  −  1 2
      □
```

**2.**

```
    □□ R4
  6)1 4 8
  −□□
    □
  −  4
    □
```

**3.** 5)‾125

**4.** 8)‾418

Name _____

# Deciding Where to Start Dividing

Complete each calculation.

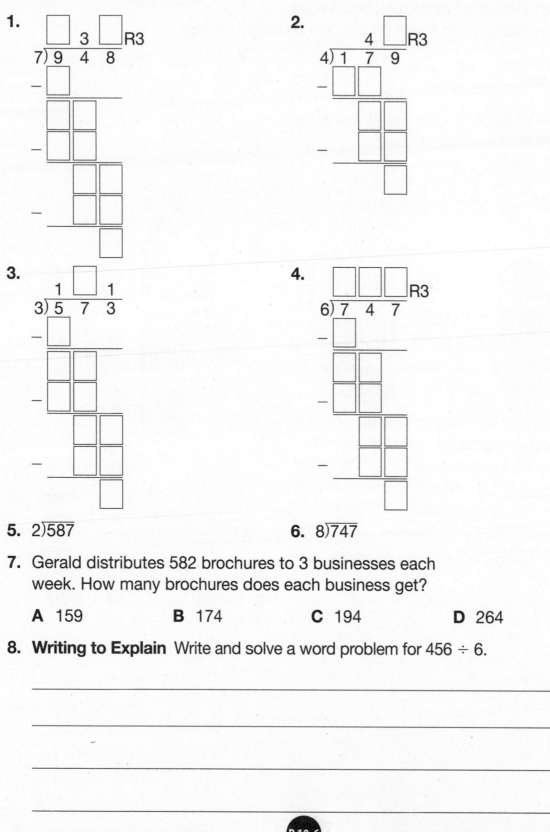

1.
$$7 \overline{)9\ 4\ 8}$$
□ 3 □ R3

2.
$$4 \overline{)1\ 7\ 9}$$
4 □ R3

3.
$$3 \overline{)5\ 7\ 3}$$
1 □ 1

4.
$$6 \overline{)7\ 4\ 7}$$
□ □ □ R3

5. 2)587

6. 8)747

7. Gerald distributes 582 brochures to 3 businesses each week. How many brochures does each business get?

**A** 159          **B** 174          **C** 194          **D** 264

8. **Writing to Explain** Write and solve a word problem for 456 ÷ 6.

_____

_____

_____

# Dividing 4-Digit by 1-Digit Numbers

An estimate will help you decide where to place the first digit of the quotient. It will also help you check your answer.

Divide 5,493 ÷ 6.

| Estimate first. You can use compatible numbers to divide mentally. | Divide to find the actual quotient. | Compare: Is the estimate close to the quotient? |
|---|---|---|
| 54 is a multiple of 6. |  | estimate: _____ |
| 5,400 is close to 5,493 and 5,400 ÷ 6 will be easy to divide. | | quotient: _____ |
| 5,400 ÷ 6 = _____ | | If it is, then your answer is reasonable. |

Estimate. Then find each quotient. Use your estimate to check if your quotient is reasonable.

**1.** Divide 4,318 ÷ 7.

Estimate:

_____ ÷ _____ = _____

4,318 ÷ 7 = _____

Is your answer reasonable?_____

**2.** Divide 4,826 ÷ 5.

Estimate:

_____ ÷ _____ = _____

4,826 ÷ 5 = _____

Is your answer reasonable?_____

**3.** Divide 4,377 ÷ 8.

Estimate:

_____ ÷ _____ = _____

4,377 ÷ 8 = _____

Is your answer reasonable?_____

**4.** Divide 7,192 ÷ 9.

Estimate:

_____ ÷ _____ = _____

7,192 ÷ 9 = _____

Is your answer reasonable?_____

Name _____

# Dividing 4-Digit by 1-Digit Numbers

Estimate. Then find each quotient. Use your estimate to check if your answer is reasonable.

1. $4\overline{)1,227}$      2. $5\overline{)2,438}$      3. $8\overline{)4,904}$

4. $7\overline{)2,611}$      5. $6\overline{)4,998}$      6. $9\overline{)3,834}$

7. $3\overline{)1,675}$      8. $4\overline{)1,254}$

9. $544 \div 8 =$ _____    10. $2,430 \div 6 =$ _____

11. At the airport, there are 1,160 seats in the waiting areas. There are 8 separate, same size, waiting areas. How many seats are in each waiting area? _____

12. A wall by the school parking lot has an area of 1,666 square feet. Seven teams of students will paint a mural on the wall. Each team will paint an equal area of the wall. How many square feet will each team paint? _____

13. **Geometry** Conner put a fence around the perimeter of his rectangular yard. The perimeter of the yard is 858 feet. Conner put a fence post in every 6 feet. How many fence posts did he use?

    **A** 142 R4      **B** 143      **C** 143 R2      **D** 153

14. Lilly estimated a quotient of 120 and found an actual quotient of 83. What should she do next? Explain.

_____

_____

_____

_____

_____

# Problem Solving: Multiple-Step Problems

## Solve Problems Step-by-Step

Scott and Gina want to go see a movie after they eat dinner. They have brought $35 with them. Scott's meal costs $9 and Gina's meal costs $8. Movie tickets are $9 each. Will they have enough money left over after dinner to pay for 2 movie tickets?

**First Step**
Write down what you know:
- They have $35 to spend.
- They are spending $9 and $8 on dinner.

**Second Step**
Write down what you need to know:
- How much money is left over?
- Is it enough for 2 movie tickets?

**Third Step**
Develop a problem-solving strategy:
- Subtract $9 and $8 from $35.
  (Tip: Instead of subtracting these from $35 one at a time, combine them and then subtract from $35.)

| $ 9 | | $35 |
|---|---|---|
| +$ 8 | then, | −$17 |
| $17.00 | | $18 |

**Fourth Step**
Finish the problem:
- Is $18 enough for 2 movie tickets that cost $9 each?
  $9 × 2 = $18
  They have $18 left. Yes, they have enough for 2 movie tickets.

Solve the problems below using the step-by-step process.

1. Nick and his friends are working on a project. They need to write 29 pages altogether. If his friend Kara writes 14 pages, and his friend Jared writes 12 pages, how many pages are left for Nick to write? _____

2. Ashlyn and Brooke went to the arcade with $18. They bought 4 bottles of water, which cost $2 each. They each bought a sticker book for $3 each. Ashlyn put $1 in a fundraiser jar. A game of pool cost $3 per game. Did they have enough money left to play? _____

3. **Reasoning** Cyndi and Jewel went shopping for school supplies. They had $14 to spend. They spent $4 on pencils, $3 on pens, and $6 on notebook paper. Cyndi thought she had enough money left over to buy a $2 pencil sharpener. Was she correct?

# Problem Solving:
# Multiple-Step Problems

Write and answer the hidden question or questions.
Then solve the problem. Write your answer in a
complete sentence.

| County Fair Admission | |
|---|---|
| Adults | $5 |
| Students | $3 |
| Children | $2 |

1. Mario and his family went to the county
   fair. They bought 2 adult passes and
   3 children's passes. What was the
   total cost for the family?

   _____

   _____

   _____

   _____

2. A bus has 12 rows with 1 seat in each row on one side and
   12 rows with 2 seats in each row on the other side. How
   many seats does the bus have altogether?

   _____

   _____

   _____

   _____

3. **Writing to Explain** Write a problem about going to the laundromat
   that has a hidden question. A single load of laundry costs $2 and a
   double load costs $4. Solve your problem.

   _____

   _____

   _____

# Factors

When multiplying two numbers, you know that both numbers are factors of the product.

## Example 1

Find the factors of 24.

Factors   Product
  ↓          ↓

$1 \times 24 = 24$
$2 \times 12 = 24$
$3 \times 8 = 24$
$4 \times 6 = 24$

Factors of 24:
1, 2, 3, 4, 6, 8, 12, and 24

## Example 2

Find the factors of 16.

What two numbers multiply together to equal 16?

$1 \times 16 = 16$
$2 \times 8 = 16$
$4 \times 4 = 16$
$8 \times 2 = 16$
$16 \times 1 = 16$

Factors of 16: 1, 2, 4, 8, and 16

List all the factors of each number.

**1.** 18

**2.** 21

**3.** 11

_____

_____

_____

**4.** 14

**5.** 23

**6.** 33

_____

_____

_____

**7. Number Sense** Irene wants to list all of the factors for the number 42. She writes 2, 3, 6, 7, 14, 21, and 42. Is she correct? Explain.

_____

_____

_____

_____

# Factors

For **1** through **12**, find all the factors of each number.

**1.** 54

**2.** 17

**3.** 28

**4.** 31

_____

_____

**5.** 44

**6.** 47

**7.** 77

**8.** 71

_____

_____

**9.** 65

**10.** 23

**11.** 57

**12.** 24

_____

_____

**13.** Karl's mother buys 60 party favors to give out as gifts during Karl's birthday party. Which number of guests will NOT let her divide the party favors evenly among the guests?

**A** 12　　　　**B** 15　　　　**C** 20　　　　**D** 25

**14. Writing to Explain** Mrs. Fisher has 91 watches on display at her store. She says she can arrange them into rows and columns without any watches left over. Mr. Fisher says that she can only make 1 row with all 91 watches. Who is right and why?

_____

_____

_____

# Prime and Composite Numbers

A **composite number** is a whole number greater than 1 that has more than two different factors. 15 has four different factors, 1, 3, 5, and 15, so 15 is a composite number.

A **prime number** is a whole number greater than 1 that has exactly two factors, itself and 1. 17 has exactly two factors, 1 and 17, so 17 is a prime number.

| **Example 1** | **Example 2** |
|---|---|
| Is 7 a prime or composite number? | Is 6 a prime or composite number? |
| Find all the factors of 7. | Find all the factors of 6. |
| Factors of 7: 1, 7 | Factors of 6: 1, 2, 3, 6 |
| 1 and 7 divide evenly into 7. | 1, 2, 3, and 6 divide evenly into 6. |
| 7 is a prime number because it only has two factors, the number itself and 1. | 6 is a composite number because it has more than two factors. |

Tell if the number is prime or composite.

**1.** 5 

**2.** 12 

**3.** 18

_____      _____      _____

**4.** 15 

**5.** 37 

**6.** 43

_____      _____      _____

Name _____

# Prime and
# Composite Numbers

In **1** through **16**, write whether each number is prime or composite.

**1.** 81

**2.** 43

**3.** 572

**4.** 63

_____  _____  _____  _____

**5.** 53

**6.** 87

**7.** 3

**8.** 27

_____  _____  _____  _____

**9.** 88

**10.** 19

**11.** 69

**12.** 79

_____  _____  _____  _____

**13.** 3,235

**14.** 1,212

**15.** 57

**16.** 17

_____  _____  _____  _____

**17.** Mr. Gerry's class has 19 students, Ms. Vernon's class has 21 students, and Mr. Singh's class has 23 students. Whose class has a composite number of students?

_____

**18.** Every prime number greater than 10 has a digit in the ones place that is included in which set of numbers below?

**A** 1, 3, 7, 9

**C** 0, 2, 4, 5, 6, 8

**B** 1, 3, 5, 9

**D** 1, 3, 7

**19. Writing to Explain** Marla says that every number in the nineties is composite. Jackie says that one number in the nineties is prime. Who is correct? Explain your answer.

_____

_____

_____

# Multiples

You can use a multiplication table to help find some multiples for numbers.

What are some multiples of 5?

**Step 1** Find the column for 5.

**Step 2** All the numbers in that column are multiples of 5.

**Tip** You could use the row for 5 instead of the column for 5.

In the chart, the multiples of 5 are 5, 10, 15, 20, 25, 30, 35, 40, and 45.

| × | 1 | 2 | 3 | 4 | 5 | 6 | 7 | 8 | 9 |
|---|---|---|---|---|---|---|---|---|---|
| 1 | 1 | 2 | 3 | 4 | (5) | 6 | 7 | 8 | 9 |
| 2 | 2 | 4 | 6 | 8 | 10 | 12 | 14 | 16 | 18 |
| 3 | 3 | 6 | 9 | 12 | 15 | 18 | 21 | 24 | 27 |
| 4 | 4 | 8 | 12 | 16 | 20 | 24 | 28 | 32 | 36 |
| 5 | 5 | 10 | 15 | 20 | 25 | 30 | 35 | 40 | 45 |
| 6 | 6 | 12 | 18 | 24 | 30 | 36 | 42 | 48 | 54 |
| 7 | 7 | 14 | 21 | 28 | 35 | 42 | 49 | 56 | 63 |
| 8 | 8 | 16 | 24 | 32 | 40 | 48 | 56 | 64 | 72 |
| 9 | 9 | 18 | 27 | 36 | 45 | 54 | 63 | 72 | 81 |

In **1** through **8**, write five multiples of each number.

**1.** 3

**2.** 7

**3.** 9

**4.** 2

_____

**5.** 1

**6.** 8

**7.** 6

**8.** 4

_____

In **9** through **12**, tell whether the first number is a multiple of the second number.

**9.** 18, 3

**10.** 24, 6

**11.** 32, 7

**12.** 12, 4

_____

**13. Number Sense** What number has 12, 24, and 30 as multiples? Explain how you found your answer.

_____

_____

_____

# Multiples

In **1** through **8**, write five multiples of each number.

**1.** 5 _____

**2.** 3 _____

**3.** 7 _____

**4.** 4 _____

**5.** 9 _____

**6.** 2 _____

**7.** 6 _____

**8.** 8 _____

In **9** through **16**, tell whether the first number is a multiple of the second number.

**9.** 21, 7 _____

**10.** 28, 3 _____

**11.** 17, 3 _____

**12.** 20, 4 _____

**13.** 54, 9 _____

**14.** 15, 5 _____

**15.** 26, 4 _____

**16.** 32, 8 _____

**17.** Circle the number in the box that is a multiple of 8.

| 10 | 18 | 20 | 24 | 31 | 36 |

**18.** **Number Sense** List five multiples for 3 and five multiples for 4. Then circle the common multiples.

_____

_____

**19.** **Reasoning** What number has factors of 2 and 3 and multiples of 12 and 18?

_____

**20.** What are five multiples of 9?

   **A** 9, 19, 29, 39, 49   **B** 9, 18, 27, 36, 45   **C** 1, 3, 9, 18, 27   **D** 1, 9, 18, 27, 36

**21.** Carmen listed the multiples of 6 as 1, 2, 3, and 6. Is she correct? Explain why or why not.

_____

_____

# Equivalent Fractions

If two fractions name the same amount, they are called
**equivalent fractions**.

Use multiplication to write a fraction equivalent to $\frac{1}{2}$.

Multiply the numerator and denominator by the same number.

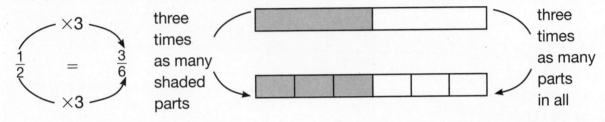

three
times
as many
shaded
parts

three
times
as many
parts
in all

$\frac{1}{2}$ and $\frac{3}{6}$ are equivalent fractions.

Use division to write a fraction that is equivalent to $\frac{10}{12}$.

Think of a number that is a factor of both 10 and 12. Two is a factor
of 10 and 12. Divide the numerator and the denominator by 2.

$\frac{10}{12} = \frac{5}{6}$   $\frac{10}{12}$ and $\frac{5}{6}$ are equivalent fractions.

---

Find the missing number.

**1.** $\frac{1}{4} = \frac{\square}{8}$ _____

**2.** $\frac{9}{12} = \frac{\square}{4}$ _____

**3.** $\frac{2}{3} = \frac{\square}{6}$ _____

**4.** $\frac{4}{5} = \frac{\square}{10}$ _____

Multiply to find an equivalent fraction.

**5.** $\frac{1}{4} =$ ___

**6.** $\frac{1}{2} =$ ___

**7.** $\frac{1}{6} =$ ___

**8.** $\frac{3}{4} =$ ___

Divide to find an equivalent fraction.

**9.** $\frac{8}{12} =$ ___

**10.** $\frac{9}{12} =$ ___

**11.** $\frac{4}{8} =$ ___

**12.** $\frac{2}{6} =$ ___

**13.** $\frac{4}{10} =$ ___

**14.** $\frac{5}{10} =$ ___

**15.** $\frac{8}{10} =$ ___

**16.** $\frac{6}{8} =$ ___

Name _____

# Equivalent Fractions

Find the missing number.

1. $\frac{1}{2} = \frac{\square}{12}$

2. $\frac{6}{10} = \frac{\square}{5}$

3. $\frac{3}{12} = \frac{\square}{4}$

4. $\frac{4}{5} = \frac{\square}{10}$

_____     _____     _____     _____

Find an equivalent fraction.

5. $\frac{1}{2}$

6. $\frac{2}{12}$

7. $\frac{6}{10}$

8. $\frac{6}{8}$

9. $\frac{8}{12}$

_____     _____     _____     _____

10. Is $\frac{2}{14}$ equivalent to $\frac{3}{7}$? _____

11. In Mark's collection of antique bottles, $\frac{1}{2}$ of the bottles
are dark green. Write three equivalent fractions for $\frac{1}{2}$.

_____

12. Write a pair of equivalent fractions for the picture below.

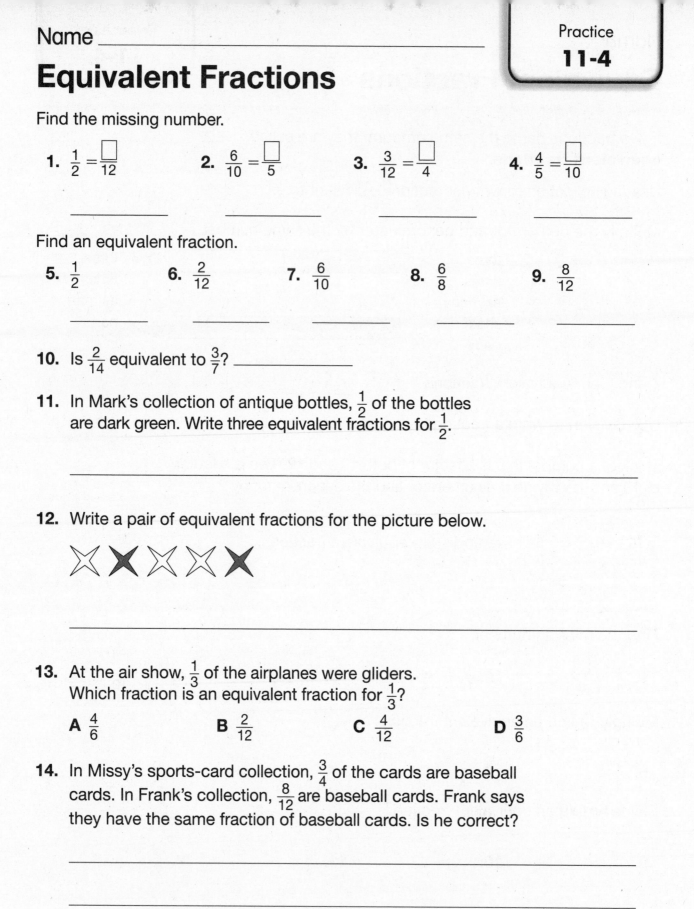

_____

13. At the air show, $\frac{1}{3}$ of the airplanes were gliders.
Which fraction is an equivalent fraction for $\frac{1}{3}$?

  **A** $\frac{4}{6}$       **B** $\frac{2}{12}$       **C** $\frac{4}{12}$       **D** $\frac{3}{6}$

14. In Missy's sports-card collection, $\frac{3}{4}$ of the cards are baseball
cards. In Frank's collection, $\frac{8}{12}$ are baseball cards. Frank says
they have the same fraction of baseball cards. Is he correct?

_____

_____

# Number Lines and Equivalent Fractions

Write two equivalent fractions that name the point on the number line.

0 ———————————————————— 1

**Step 1** Count the number of tick marks from 0 to 1.

On this number line, there are 12. That tells you the denominator of one fraction is 12.

**Step 2** Count the number of tick marks from 0 to where the point is.

There are 8. That tells you the numerator of the fraction is 8. You now know one fraction that names the point is $\frac{8}{12}$.

**Step 3** 12 is an even number, so it can be divided by 2.

$12 \div 2 = 6$

If you count every second tick mark from 0 to 1, you will count 6 tick marks. The denominator of another fraction is 6.

Now, count every second tick mark from 0 to the location of the point. There are 4, so the numerator of the fraction is 4. An equivalent fraction to $\frac{8}{12}$ is $\frac{4}{6}$.

$$\frac{8}{12} = \frac{4}{6}$$

Write two fractions that name the point on the number line.

1.

0 ——————————————— 1

_____

2.

0 ——————————————— 1

_____

3. **Draw a Diagram** Are $\frac{3}{8}$ and $\frac{3}{4}$ equivalent fractions? Draw a number line to show your answer.

_____

_____

_____

# Number Lines and Equivalent Fractions

Write two fractions that name each point on the
number line.

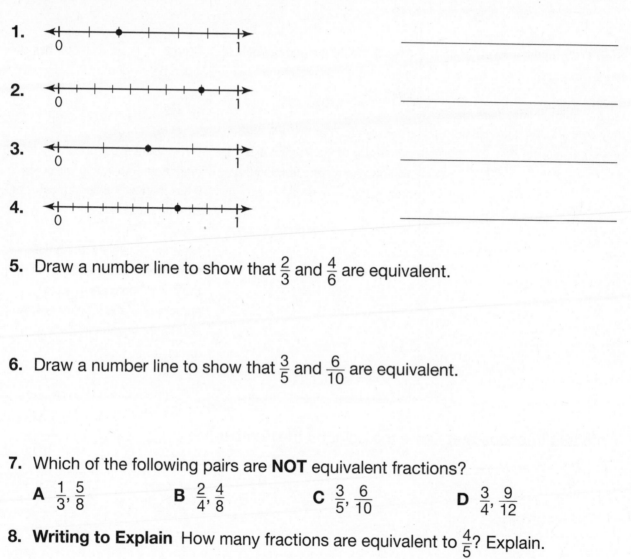

**1.**    0          1              _____

**2.**    0          1              _____

**3.**    0          1              _____

**4.**    0          1              _____

**5.** Draw a number line to show that $\frac{2}{3}$ and $\frac{4}{6}$ are equivalent.

**6.** Draw a number line to show that $\frac{3}{5}$ and $\frac{6}{10}$ are equivalent.

**7.** Which of the following pairs are **NOT** equivalent fractions?

  **A** $\frac{1}{3}, \frac{5}{8}$        **B** $\frac{2}{4}, \frac{4}{8}$        **C** $\frac{3}{5}, \frac{6}{10}$        **D** $\frac{3}{4}, \frac{9}{12}$

**8. Writing to Explain** How many fractions are equivalent to $\frac{4}{5}$? Explain.

_____

_____

_____

_____

# Comparing Fractions

Leanne wanted to compare $\frac{4}{6}$ and $\frac{3}{4}$. She used fraction strips to help.

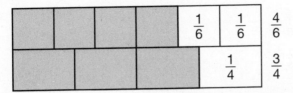

She compared the amounts that were shaded in each picture. Because the amount shaded in $\frac{3}{4}$ is more than the amount shaded in $\frac{4}{6}$, she knew that $\frac{3}{4}$ is greater than $\frac{4}{6}$.

So, $\frac{3}{4} > \frac{4}{6}$.

Write > or < for each $\bigcirc$. Use fraction strips or benchmark fractions to help.

**1.** $\frac{5}{6}$ $\bigcirc$ $\frac{2}{3}$      **2.** $\frac{1}{5}$ $\bigcirc$ $\frac{2}{8}$      **3.** $\frac{9}{10}$ $\bigcirc$ $\frac{6}{8}$      **4.** $\frac{3}{4}$ $\bigcirc$ $\frac{1}{4}$

**5.** $\frac{7}{8}$ $\bigcirc$ $\frac{5}{10}$      **6.** $\frac{2}{5}$ $\bigcirc$ $\frac{2}{6}$      **7.** $\frac{1}{3}$ $\bigcirc$ $\frac{3}{8}$      **8.** $\frac{2}{10}$ $\bigcirc$ $\frac{3}{5}$

The same number of students attended school all week.

| Day | Fraction of students buying lunch |
|---|---|
| Monday | $\frac{1}{2}$ |
| Tuesday | $\frac{2}{5}$ |
| Wednesday | $\frac{3}{4}$ |
| Thursday | $\frac{5}{8}$ |
| Friday | $\frac{4}{6}$ |

**9.** Did more students buy lunch on Tuesday or on Wednesday?

_____

**10.** Did more students buy lunch on Thursday or on Friday?

_____

Name _____

# Comparing Fractions

Write > or < for each ◯. You may use fraction strips to help.

1. $\frac{1}{2}$ ◯ $\frac{3}{10}$    2. $\frac{8}{12}$ ◯ $\frac{5}{12}$    3. $\frac{3}{8}$ ◯ $\frac{1}{2}$

4. $\frac{3}{3}$ ◯ $\frac{7}{8}$    5. $\frac{3}{5}$ ◯ $\frac{1}{3}$    6. $\frac{1}{4}$ ◯ $\frac{2}{4}$

7. $\frac{5}{6}$ ◯ $\frac{5}{8}$    8. $\frac{7}{12}$ ◯ $\frac{4}{5}$    9. $\frac{3}{10}$ ◯ $\frac{6}{10}$

10. **Number Sense** Explain how you know that $\frac{21}{30}$ is greater than $\frac{2}{3}$.

_____

_____

_____

11. Tina completed $\frac{2}{3}$ of her homework.
George completed $\frac{7}{8}$ of his homework.
Who completed a greater fraction of homework?  _____

12. Jackson played a video game for $\frac{1}{6}$ hour. Hailey played
a video game for $\frac{1}{3}$ hour. Who played the video game
for a greater amount of time?  _____

13. Which fraction is greater than $\frac{3}{4}$?

   A $\frac{1}{2}$        B $\frac{2}{5}$        C $\frac{5}{8}$        D $\frac{7}{8}$

14. **Writing to Explain** James says that $\frac{5}{5}$ is greater than $\frac{9}{10}$.
Is he correct? Explain.

_____

_____

_____

_____

# Ordering Fractions

How can you order fractions?

Order $\frac{2}{3}$, $\frac{1}{6}$, $\frac{7}{12}$ from least to greatest.

| $\frac{1}{3}$ | | | $\frac{1}{3}$ | | | $\frac{1}{3}$ | | |
|---|---|---|---|---|---|---|---|---|
| $\frac{1}{6}$ | $\frac{1}{6}$ | $\frac{1}{6}$ | $\frac{1}{6}$ | $\frac{1}{6}$ | $\frac{1}{6}$ | | | |
| $\frac{1}{12}$ | $\frac{1}{12}$ | $\frac{1}{12}$ | $\frac{1}{12}$ | $\frac{1}{12}$ | $\frac{1}{12}$ | $\frac{1}{12}$ | $\frac{1}{12}$ | $\frac{1}{12}$ $\frac{1}{12}$ $\frac{1}{12}$ $\frac{1}{12}$ |

Find equivalent fractions with a common denominator.

| $\frac{1}{12}$ | $\frac{1}{12}$ | $\frac{1}{12}$ | $\frac{1}{12}$ | $\frac{1}{12}$ | $\frac{1}{12}$ | $\frac{1}{12}$ | $\frac{1}{12}$ |
| $\frac{1}{12}$ | $\frac{1}{12}$ |
| $\frac{1}{12}$ | $\frac{1}{12}$ | $\frac{1}{12}$ | $\frac{1}{12}$ | $\frac{1}{12}$ | $\frac{1}{12}$ | $\frac{1}{12}$ |

Compare the numerators.
Order the fractions from least to greatest.
$\frac{2}{12} < \frac{7}{12} < \frac{8}{12}$.

Order the fractions from least to greatest.

**1.** $\frac{3}{10}$, $\frac{3}{6}$, $\frac{2}{5}$

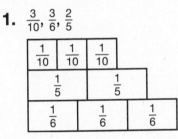

**2.** $\frac{3}{8}$, $\frac{1}{3}$, $\frac{3}{12}$

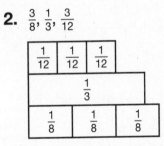

Find equivalent fractions with a common denominator and order from least to greatest.

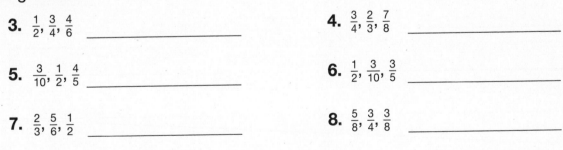

**3.** $\frac{1}{2}$, $\frac{3}{4}$, $\frac{4}{6}$ _____

**4.** $\frac{3}{4}$, $\frac{2}{3}$, $\frac{7}{8}$ _____

**5.** $\frac{3}{10}$, $\frac{1}{2}$, $\frac{4}{5}$ _____

**6.** $\frac{1}{2}$, $\frac{3}{10}$, $\frac{3}{5}$ _____

**7.** $\frac{2}{3}$, $\frac{5}{6}$, $\frac{1}{2}$ _____

**8.** $\frac{5}{8}$, $\frac{3}{4}$, $\frac{3}{8}$ _____

Name _____

# Ordering Fractions

Order the fractions from least to greatest.

**1.** $\frac{3}{5}, \frac{7}{8}, \frac{5}{6}$

**2.** $\frac{1}{2}, \frac{7}{12}, \frac{4}{10}$

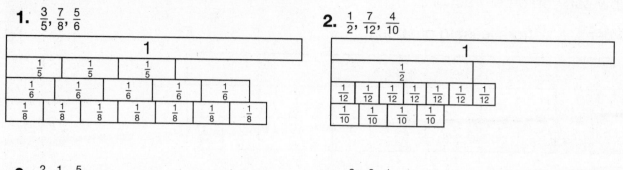

**3.** $\frac{2}{6}, \frac{1}{4}, \frac{5}{12}$

**4.** $\frac{3}{10}, \frac{2}{5}, \frac{1}{3}$

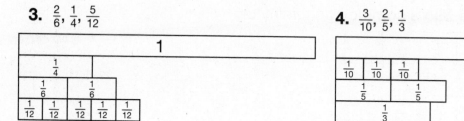

Find equivalent fractions with a common denominator and order from least to greatest.

**5.** $\frac{2}{3}, \frac{1}{2}, \frac{5}{12}$ _____

**6.** $\frac{1}{6}, \frac{1}{3}, \frac{3}{4}$ _____

**7.** $\frac{5}{6}, \frac{2}{3}, \frac{3}{4}$ _____

**8.** $\frac{7}{12}, \frac{2}{6}, \frac{1}{4}$ _____

**9.** $\frac{4}{5}, \frac{3}{10}, \frac{1}{2}$ _____

**10.** $\frac{9}{12}, \frac{1}{3}, \frac{3}{6}$ _____

**11.** Which fraction is greater than $\frac{2}{3}$?

**A** $\frac{1}{12}$      **B** $\frac{2}{6}$      **C** $\frac{5}{12}$      **D** $\frac{6}{8}$

**12.** **Writing to Explain** Explain how you know that $\frac{7}{12}$ is greater than $\frac{1}{3}$ but less than $\frac{2}{3}$?

_____

_____

_____

_____

# Problem Solving:
# Writing to Explain

Gina and her brother Don made homemade pasta with their mother. Gina made $\frac{1}{4}$ of a pan of pasta. Don made $\frac{3}{8}$ of a pan. Which person made more pasta?

**Writing to Explain**

- Write your explanation in steps to make it clear.

- Tell what the numbers mean in your explanation.

- Tell why you took certain steps.

**Example**

- Because $\frac{1}{4}$ and $\frac{3}{8}$ have different denominators, I multiplied the numerator and denominator of $\frac{1}{4}$ by 2 to get $\frac{2}{8}$.

- Then I could compare the numerators of $\frac{2}{8}$ and $\frac{3}{8}$. Because $\frac{3}{8}$ is greater than $\frac{2}{8}$ I knew that Don made more pasta.

1. Rick has a collection of 6 video games. He lets his best friend borrow $\frac{2}{6}$ of his video game collection. Write two fractions equivalent to this number. Explain how you came up with the fractions.

_____

_____

_____

_____

_____

Name _____

# Problem Solving: Writing to Explain

1. Mary has 12 marbles. $\frac{3}{12}$ of the marbles are yellow and $\frac{2}{12}$ of the marbles are blue. The rest of the marbles are green. How many marbles are green? Explain how you know.

_____

_____

_____

_____

_____

2. Adam wants to compare the fractions $\frac{3}{12}$, $\frac{1}{6}$, and $\frac{1}{3}$. He wants to order them from least to greatest and rewrite them so they all have the same denominator. Explain how Adam can rewrite the fractions.

_____

_____

_____

_____

3. Adam used the three fractions to make a circle graph and colored each a different color. What fraction of the graph is not colored? Explain your answer.

_____

_____

_____

# Modeling Addition of Fractions

Eight friends want to see a movie. Four of them want to see a comedy. Two want to see an action movie and two want to see a science-fiction movie. What fraction of the group wants to see either a comedy or a science-fiction movie?

You can use a model to add fractions.

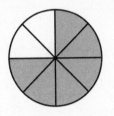

Look at the circle. It is divided into eighths, because there are eight people in the group. Each person represents $\frac{1}{8}$ of the group. Four people want to see a comedy. Shade in four of the sections to represent $\frac{4}{8}$. Two people want to see a science-fiction movie. Shade in two more sections to represent $\frac{2}{8}$. Count the number of shaded sections. There are six. So, $\frac{6}{8}$ of the group wants to see either a comedy or a science fiction movie.

$\frac{4}{8} + \frac{2}{8} = \frac{6}{8}$   Write the sum in simplest form.   $\frac{6 \div 2}{8 \div 2} = \frac{3}{4}$

Find each sum. Simplify, if possible.

1. $\frac{2}{5} + \frac{1}{5}$ _____

2. $\frac{4}{6} + \frac{1}{6}$ _____

3. $\frac{3}{8} + \frac{3}{8}$ _____

4. $\frac{1}{6} + \frac{1}{6}$ _____

5. $\frac{2}{5} + \frac{3}{5}$ _____

6. $\frac{2}{10} + \frac{3}{10}$ _____

7. $\frac{5}{8} + \frac{3}{8}$ _____

8. $\frac{3}{10} + \frac{1}{10}$ _____

9. $\frac{3}{4} + \frac{1}{4}$ _____

10. $\frac{5}{10} + \frac{4}{10}$ _____

11. $\frac{1}{6} + \frac{1}{6} + \frac{1}{6}$ _____

12. $\frac{1}{12} + \frac{5}{12} + \frac{2}{12}$ _____

13. **Number Sense** We can express time as a fraction of an hour. For example, 15 minutes is $\frac{1}{4}$ hour. 30 minutes is $\frac{1}{2}$ hour. What fraction of an hour is 45 minutes? _____

R 12·1

Name _____

# Modeling Addition of Fractions

Find each sum. Simplify if possible. You may use fraction strips.

1. $\frac{1}{4} + \frac{1}{4}$ _____

2. $\frac{2}{5} + \frac{1}{5}$ _____

3. $\frac{3}{12} + \frac{1}{12}$ _____

4. $\frac{2}{6} + \frac{3}{6}$ _____

5. $\frac{1}{2} + \frac{2}{2}$ _____

6. $\frac{2}{8} + \frac{5}{8}$ _____

7. $\frac{3}{8} + \frac{3}{8}$ _____

8. $\frac{3}{10} + \frac{2}{10}$ _____

9. $\frac{1}{6} + \frac{2}{6}$ _____

10. **Draw a Picture** A rectangular garden is divided into 10 equal parts. Draw a picture that shows $\frac{3}{10} + \frac{3}{10} = \frac{6}{10}$, or $\frac{3}{5}$.

11. Each day, Steven walked $\frac{1}{12}$ mile more than the previous day. The first day he walked $\frac{1}{12}$, the second day he walked $\frac{2}{12}$ mile, the third day he walked $\frac{3}{12}$ mile. On which day did the sum of his walks total at least 1 complete mile?

_____

12. **Algebra** Find the missing value in the equation.

$\frac{3}{12} + \frac{1}{12} + \frac{?}{12} = \frac{1}{2}$

**A** 1          **B** 2          **C** 3          **D** 4

13. There are five people sitting around the dinner table. Each person has $\frac{2}{10}$ of a pie on their plate. How much pie is left? Explain.

_____

_____

_____

# Adding Fractions with Like Denominators

When you add fractions with like denominators, add the numerators and keep the denominator the same.

Find the sum of $\frac{3}{8} + \frac{1}{8}$

Add the numerators. $3 + 1 = 4$

Keep the denominator the same. $\frac{3}{8} + \frac{1}{8} = \frac{4}{8}$

Is this fraction expressed in simplest form?

**Remember:** a fraction is in simplest form when the greatest common factor (GCF) of the numerator and denominator is 1.

$\frac{4 \div 4}{8 \div 4} = \frac{1}{2}$    $\frac{1}{2}$ is in simplest form, because the GCF of 1 and 2 is 1.

Find each sum. Simplify if possible.

**1.** $\frac{1}{3} + \frac{1}{3}$

_____

**2.** $\frac{3}{10} + \frac{6}{10}$

_____

**3.** $\frac{5}{12} + \frac{2}{12}$

_____

**4.** $\frac{3}{12} + \frac{7}{12}$

_____

**5.** $\frac{5}{10} + \frac{3}{10}$

_____

**6.** $\frac{2}{8} + \frac{4}{8}$

_____

**7.** $\frac{7}{10} + \frac{3}{10}$

_____

**8.** $\frac{1}{8} + \frac{6}{8}$

_____

**9.** $\frac{1}{10} + \frac{5}{10}$

_____

**10.** $\frac{1}{5} + \frac{2}{5} + \frac{2}{5}$

_____

**11.** $\frac{2}{8} + \frac{1}{8} + \frac{4}{8}$

_____

**12.** $\frac{2}{6} + \frac{1}{6}$

_____

**13. Reasoning** There were 10 bowling pins standing before Jared took his first turn. On his first turn, he knocked down 5 pins. On his second turn, he knocked down 3 pins. What fraction of the pins did Jared knock down in his two turns?

_____

# Adding Fractions with Like Denominators

Find each sum. Simplify if possible.

**1.** $\frac{2}{5} + \frac{2}{5}$

_____

**2.** $\frac{4}{10} + \frac{5}{10}$

_____

**3.** $\frac{3}{8} + \frac{1}{8}$

_____

**4.** $\frac{3}{6} + \frac{2}{6}$

_____

**5.** $\frac{2}{10} + \frac{7}{10}$

_____

**6.** $\frac{5}{8} + \frac{2}{8}$

_____

**7.** $\frac{1}{6} + \frac{2}{6}$

_____

**8.** $\frac{9}{12} + \frac{2}{12}$

_____

**9.** $\frac{4}{12} + \frac{6}{12}$

_____

**10.** $\frac{2}{12} + \frac{9}{12}$

_____

**11.** $\frac{1}{8} + \frac{3}{8} + \frac{2}{8}$

_____

**12.** $\frac{2}{10} + \frac{1}{10} + \frac{5}{10}$

_____

**13.** $\frac{4}{12} + \frac{2}{12} + \frac{1}{12}$

_____

**14.** $\frac{2}{5} + \frac{1}{5} + \frac{1}{5}$

_____

**15. Geometry** A side of an equilateral triangle is $\frac{2}{8}$ cm long. Draw a picture that shows the triangle. What is the perimeter of the triangle? _____

**16.** Of the computer games Lynne owns, $\frac{5}{12}$ are sport games and $\frac{3}{12}$ are educational. What fraction of the games are either sport games or educational games?

**A** $\frac{4}{12}$      **B** $\frac{1}{2}$      **C** $\frac{2}{3}$      **D** $\frac{3}{4}$

**17.** Rob and Nancy are working on a project. Rob completes $\frac{1}{8}$ of it on Monday and $\frac{3}{8}$ of it on Tuesday. Nancy completes $\frac{2}{8}$ of it on Wednesday and $\frac{1}{8}$ of it on Thursday. Is the project complete? Explain.

_____

_____

# Modeling Subtraction of Fractions

Karla made a pizza and cut it into 10 slices. She ate two slices.
What fraction of the pizza is left?

You can use a model to subtract fractions.

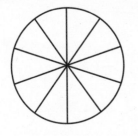

Karla's pizza is divided into 10 slices. One way to show
this is $\frac{10}{10} = 1$ whole pizza. Karla ate two slices of the pizza.
Cross out two of the slices. Count the number of slices left.
There are 8 slices or $\frac{8}{10}$ of the pizza left.

$$\frac{10}{10} - \frac{2}{10} = \frac{8}{10}$$

Write the answer in simplest form, if possible.

$$\frac{8 \div 2}{10 \div 2} = \frac{4}{5}$$

Use fraction strips or models to subtract. Simplify if possible.

**1.** $\frac{5}{5} - \frac{2}{5} =$ _____

**2.** $\frac{7}{10} - \frac{3}{10} =$ _____

**3.** $\frac{3}{4} - \frac{2}{4} =$ _____

**4.** $\frac{8}{10} - \frac{5}{10} =$ _____

**5.** $\frac{6}{6} - \frac{3}{6} =$ _____

**6.** $\frac{11}{12} - \frac{7}{12} =$ _____

**7.** $\frac{5}{6} - \frac{2}{6} =$ _____

**8.** $\frac{4}{8} - \frac{2}{8} =$ _____

**9.** $\frac{11}{12} - \frac{8}{12} =$ _____

**10.** $\frac{7}{12} - \frac{5}{12} =$ _____

**11.** $\frac{6}{10} - \frac{4}{10} =$ _____

**12.** $\frac{9}{12} - \frac{6}{12} =$ _____

**13. Algebra** Find x.

$$x - \frac{1}{6} = \frac{1}{6}$$ _____

# Name _____

# Modeling Subtraction of Fractions

Use fraction strips to subtract. Simplify if possible.

1. $\frac{11}{12} - \frac{5}{12}$ _____

2. $\frac{6}{12} - \frac{4}{12}$ _____

3. $\frac{1}{2} - \frac{1}{2}$ _____

4. $\frac{4}{6} - \frac{1}{6}$ _____

5. $\frac{5}{6} - \frac{4}{6}$ _____

6. $\frac{9}{10} - \frac{3}{10}$ _____

7. $\frac{5}{8} - \frac{2}{8}$ _____

8. $\frac{7}{8} - \frac{5}{8}$ _____

9. $\frac{3}{4} - \frac{2}{4}$ _____

10. $\frac{3}{5} - \frac{2}{5}$ _____

11. $\frac{2}{5} - \frac{1}{5}$ _____

12. $\frac{9}{12} - \frac{1}{12}$ _____

13. **Algebra** Evaluate $\frac{5}{8} - ? = \frac{3}{8}$. _____

14. **Draw a Diagram** Harriet has $\frac{3}{4}$ tank of gas left in her car. If she needs $\frac{1}{4}$ tank to go to her friend's house and another $\frac{1}{4}$ tank to get back home, does she have enough gas? Draw a diagram and explain your answer.

_____

_____

15. Alicia had $\frac{10}{12}$ yard of fabric. She used $\frac{8}{12}$ for a pillow. How much fabric did she have left? Explain how you found your answer.

_____

_____

# Subtracting Fractions with Like Denominators

When subtracting with two fractions having the same denominator, the difference also has the same denominator.

Find $\frac{7}{8} - \frac{5}{8}$.

**Step 1:**
Subtract the numerators.

$7 - 5 = 2$

**Step 2:**
Write the difference over the same denominator.

$\frac{7}{8} - \frac{5}{8} = \frac{2}{8}$

**Step 3:**
Simplify the answer if possible.

$\frac{2}{8} = \frac{1}{4}$

So, $\frac{7}{8} - \frac{5}{8} = \frac{1}{4}$.

Subtract the fractions. Simplify if possible.

1. $\frac{4}{5} - \frac{3}{5}$ _____

2. $\frac{8}{12} - \frac{3}{12}$ _____

3. $\frac{3}{6} - \frac{1}{6}$ _____

4. $\frac{9}{10} - \frac{3}{10}$ _____

5. $\frac{11}{12} - \frac{5}{12}$ _____

6. $\frac{5}{6} - \frac{1}{6}$ _____

7. $\frac{97}{100} - \frac{40}{100}$ _____

8. $\frac{5}{8} - \frac{1}{8}$ _____

9. $\frac{7}{10} - \frac{2}{10} - \frac{1}{10}$ _____

10. $\frac{7}{12} - \frac{4}{12}$ _____

11. $\frac{3}{4} - \frac{1}{4} - \frac{2}{4}$ _____

12. $\frac{8}{8} - \frac{1}{8}$ _____

13. **Reasoning** During archery practice, Manny hit the target 7 times out of 10 tries. What fraction of his arrows did NOT hit the target?

_____

Name _____

# Subtracting Fractions with Like Denominators

In **1** through **12**, find each difference. Simplify if possible.

1. $\frac{4}{5} - \frac{1}{5}$ _____

2. $\frac{9}{10} - \frac{5}{10}$ _____

3. $\frac{5}{8} - \frac{2}{8}$ _____

4. $\frac{6}{8} - \frac{2}{8}$ _____

5. $\frac{9}{10} - \frac{8}{10}$ _____

6. $\frac{9}{12} - \frac{5}{12}$ _____

7. $\frac{5}{6} - \frac{3}{6}$ _____

8. $\frac{3}{4} - \frac{1}{4}$ _____

9. $\frac{6}{8} - \frac{4}{8}$ _____

10. $\frac{7}{12} - \frac{3}{12}$ _____

11. $\frac{10}{12} - \frac{6}{12}$ _____

12. $\frac{4}{6} - \frac{4}{6}$ _____

13. **Geometry** The area of rectangle $A$ is $\frac{11}{12}$ square meters. The area of rectangle $B$ is $\frac{8}{12}$ square meters. How much larger is rectangle $A$?

_____

14. Joan counted that $\frac{2}{10}$ of her jelly beans were red. Dean counted that $\frac{6}{10}$ of his jelly beans were red. How much greater a fraction of Dean's jelly beans were red?

_____

15. **Think About the Process** On the weekends, Paul jogs $\frac{9}{10}$ mile. On the weekdays, Paul jogs $\frac{5}{10}$ mile. Which expression shows how many more miles Paul jogs on the weekends than on a weekday?

**A** $\frac{9}{10} + \frac{5}{10}$      **B** $\frac{9}{10} - \frac{5}{10}$      **C** $\frac{5}{10} + \frac{9}{10}$      **D** $\frac{5}{10} - \frac{9}{10}$

16. In a classroom, $\frac{2}{12}$ of the students play baseball, $\frac{4}{12}$ play football, $\frac{1}{12}$ are in the chorus, and the rest participate in volunteer programs. What fraction of the students participate in volunteer programs? Explain your answer.

_____

_____

_____

_____

Name _____

# Adding and Subtracting on the Number Line

Bernadette has $\frac{7}{8}$ yard of ribbon. She cuts off $\frac{3}{8}$ yard to make a collar for her dog. How much ribbon does Bernadette have left?

You can use a number line to help you subtract fractions.

Draw a number line to represent the ribbon. Divide the number line into eighths. Place a point at $\frac{7}{8}$ to show the length of the ribbon before it is cut. Draw an arrow $\frac{3}{8}$ of a unit to the left to show how much of the ribbon Bernadette cut off.

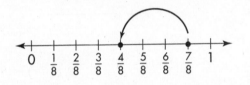

$\frac{7}{8} - \frac{3}{8} = \frac{4}{8}$   Simplify: $\frac{4}{8} = \frac{1}{2}$   There is $\frac{1}{2}$ yard of ribbon left.

You can also use a number line to help you add fractions.

Kevin and Duane are recycling aluminum cans. Each boy has collected $\frac{4}{10}$ pound. How many pounds have they collected in all?

Divide this number line into tenths. Start at zero and draw an arrow to and place a point at $\frac{4}{10}$ to show the amount of aluminum Kevin collected. Now draw another arrow $\frac{4}{10}$ of a unit long to the right to show Duane's amount.

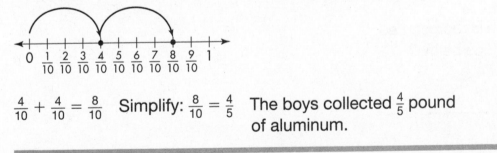

$\frac{4}{10} + \frac{4}{10} = \frac{8}{10}$   Simplify: $\frac{8}{10} = \frac{4}{5}$   The boys collected $\frac{4}{5}$ pound of aluminum.

Add or subtract the fractions. You may use a number line. Simplify your answer, if possible.

**1.** $\frac{2}{5} + \frac{1}{5} = $ _____

**2.** $\frac{8}{12} - \frac{3}{12} = $ _____

**3.** $\frac{5}{10} - \frac{3}{10} = $ _____

**4.** $\frac{2}{6} + \frac{1}{6} = $ _____

**5.** $\frac{29}{100} - \frac{4}{100} = $ _____

**6.** $\frac{1}{8} + \frac{2}{8} + \frac{3}{8} = $ _____

R 12·5

Name _____

# Adding and Subtracting on the Number Line

Write the equation shown by each number line.
Write your answer. Simplify if possible.

**1.**

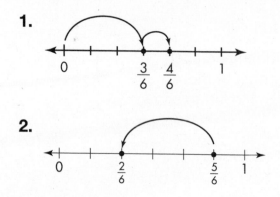

_____

**2.**

_____

Draw a number line to solve. Simplify if possible.

**3.** $\frac{3}{8} + \frac{2}{8}$ _____

**4.** $\frac{9}{12} - \frac{3}{12}$ _____

**5. Draw a Diagram** Ann is growing two different plants for a science project. Plant A grew $\frac{4}{12}$ inch the first week and $\frac{2}{12}$ inch the second week. Plant B grew $\frac{7}{12}$ inch the first week and did not grow after that. Show the heights of each plant on a different number line. Which plant is taller now?

_____

**6.** Which equation is represented by the number line below?

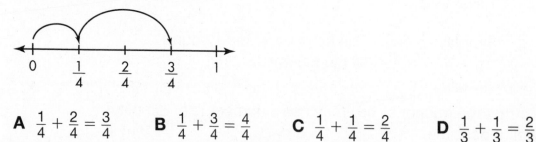

**A** $\frac{1}{4} + \frac{2}{4} = \frac{3}{4}$    **B** $\frac{1}{4} + \frac{3}{4} = \frac{4}{4}$    **C** $\frac{1}{4} + \frac{1}{4} = \frac{2}{4}$    **D** $\frac{1}{3} + \frac{1}{3} = \frac{2}{3}$

**7.** Dave made fruit punch for his party but accidentally tripped and spilled $\frac{5}{12}$ of the punch. How much of the punch was left? Explain how you found your answer.

_____

# Improper Fractions and Mixed Numbers

You can use fraction strips to write a mixed number as an improper fraction.

$3\frac{1}{2}$ of the model below is shaded.

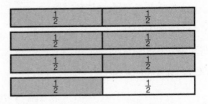

Into how many parts is each strip divided? 2. This is your denominator.

Count the shaded halves. There are 7. This is your numerator.

$3\frac{1}{2}$ is the same as the improper fraction $\frac{7}{2}$.

You can also use fraction strips to write an improper fraction as a mixed number.

$\frac{8}{3}$ of the model below is shaded.

How many strips are completely shaded? 2. This is your whole number.

What fraction of the third strip is shaded? $\frac{2}{3}$. This is your fraction.

$\frac{8}{3}$ is the same as the mixed number $2\frac{2}{3}$.

Write each mixed number as an improper fraction.

**1.** $2\frac{1}{3}$ _____

**2.** $4\frac{1}{5}$ _____

**3.** $2\frac{3}{4}$ _____

**4.** $5\frac{2}{6}$ _____

Write each improper fraction as a mixed number or a whole number.

**5.** $\frac{13}{12}$ _____

**6.** $\frac{50}{10}$ _____

**7.** $\frac{23}{10}$ _____

**8.** $\frac{17}{8}$ _____

**9. Writing to Explain** Is $\frac{45}{5}$ equal to a whole number or a mixed number? Explain how you know.

_____

_____

_____

_____

# Improper Fractions and Mixed Numbers

Write each mixed number as an improper fraction.

1. $3\frac{2}{5}$ _____
2. $6\frac{1}{4}$ _____
3. $2\frac{1}{12}$ _____
4. $2\frac{7}{10}$ _____

Write each improper fraction as a mixed number or whole number.

5. $\frac{12}{5}$ _____
6. $\frac{24}{3}$ _____
7. $\frac{32}{3}$ _____
8. $\frac{20}{12}$ _____

9. **Number Sense** Matt had to write $3\frac{4}{12}$ as an improper fraction. Write how you would tell Matt the easiest way to do so.

_____

_____

_____

_____

10. Jill has $\frac{11}{8}$ ounces of trail mix. Write the weight of Jill's trail mix as a mixed number. _____

11. Nick had $1\frac{3}{4}$ gal of milk. Write the amount of milk Nick has as an improper fraction. _____

12. Which is **NOT** an improper fraction equal to 8?

   A  $\frac{24}{3}$          B  $\frac{42}{6}$          C  $\frac{32}{4}$          D  $\frac{64}{8}$

13. **Writing to Explain** Write three different improper fractions that equal $4\frac{1}{2}$. (Hint: find equivalent fractions.)

_____

_____

# Modeling Addition and Subtraction of Mixed Numbers

**Example 1:** Draw a model to add $1\frac{7}{8} + 2\frac{3}{8}$.

**Step 1** Model each mixed number using fraction strips.

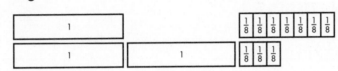

**Step 2** Add the fractions. Regroup if you can.

$$\begin{array}{r} \frac{7}{8} \\ + \frac{3}{8} \\ \hline \frac{10}{8} = 1\frac{2}{8} \end{array}$$

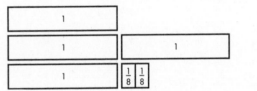

**Step 3** Add the whole numbers to the regrouped fractions. Write the sum. Simplify, if possible.

So, $1\frac{7}{8} + 2\frac{3}{8} = 4\frac{1}{4}$.

**Example 2:** Draw a model to subtract $2\frac{1}{5} - 1\frac{2}{5}$.

**Step 1** Model the number you are subtracting from, $2\frac{1}{5}$.

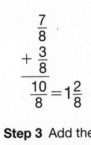

**Step 2** Rename $2\frac{1}{5}$ as $1\frac{6}{5}$. Cross out one whole and $\frac{2}{5}$ to show subtracting $1\frac{2}{5}$.

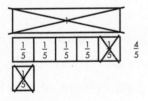

Express the part of the model that is not crossed out as a fraction or mixed number. So, $2\frac{1}{5} - 1\frac{2}{5} = \frac{4}{5}$.

Use fraction strips to find each sum or difference. Simplify, if possible.

**1.** $3\frac{1}{2} + 1\frac{1}{2}$

**2.** $2\frac{5}{8} + 4\frac{3}{8}$

**3.** $5\frac{2}{6} + 3\frac{5}{6}$

**4.** $2\frac{2}{4} + 6\frac{3}{4}$

**5.** $6\frac{1}{8} - 3\frac{5}{8}$

**6.** $8\frac{3}{12} - 2\frac{5}{12}$

**7.** $12\frac{1}{3} - 5\frac{2}{3}$

**8.** $9\frac{7}{10} - 6\frac{9}{10}$

# Modeling Addition and Subtraction of Mixed Numbers

For **1** and **2**, use each model to find each sum or difference.

**1.** $1\frac{3}{8} + 1\frac{7}{8}$

**2.** $3\frac{1}{5} - 1\frac{4}{5}$

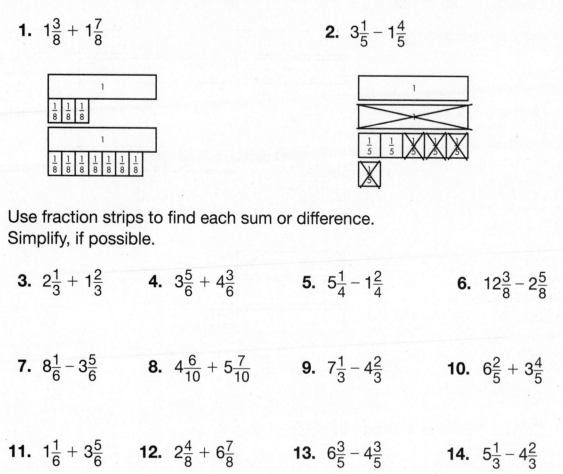

Use fraction strips to find each sum or difference.
Simplify, if possible.

**3.** $2\frac{1}{3} + 1\frac{2}{3}$

**4.** $3\frac{5}{6} + 4\frac{3}{6}$

**5.** $5\frac{1}{4} - 1\frac{2}{4}$

**6.** $12\frac{3}{8} - 2\frac{5}{8}$

**7.** $8\frac{1}{6} - 3\frac{5}{6}$

**8.** $4\frac{6}{10} + 5\frac{7}{10}$

**9.** $7\frac{1}{3} - 4\frac{2}{3}$

**10.** $6\frac{2}{5} + 3\frac{4}{5}$

**11.** $1\frac{1}{6} + 3\frac{5}{6}$

**12.** $2\frac{4}{8} + 6\frac{7}{8}$

**13.** $6\frac{3}{5} - 4\frac{3}{5}$

**14.** $5\frac{1}{3} - 4\frac{2}{3}$

**15.** Jerome's rain gauge showed $13\frac{9}{10}$ centimeters (cm) at the end of last month. At the end of this month, the rain gauge showed $15\frac{3}{10}$ centimeters. How many more centimeters of rain fell this month?

**A** $29\frac{2}{10}$ cm     **B** $15\frac{3}{10}$ cm     **C** $2\frac{4}{10}$ cm     **D** $1\frac{4}{10}$ cm

**16.** You are adding $3\frac{2}{3} + 2\frac{2}{3}$ using fraction strips. Explain how you rename the fraction part of the problem.

_____

_____

# Adding Mixed Numbers

Randy talks on the telephone for $2\frac{5}{6}$ hours, and then surfs the Internet for $3\frac{3}{4}$ hours. How many hours does he spend on the two activities?

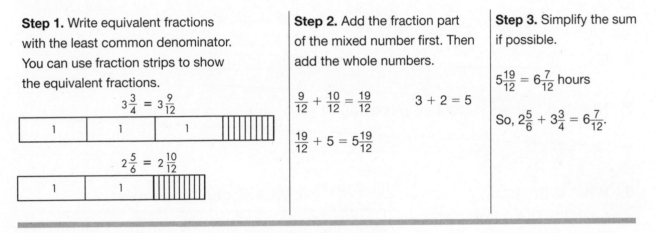

**Step 1.** Write equivalent fractions with the least common denominator. You can use fraction strips to show the equivalent fractions.

$3\frac{3}{4} = 3\frac{9}{12}$

| 1 | 1 | 1 | |

$2\frac{5}{6} = 2\frac{10}{12}$

| 1 | 1 | |

**Step 2.** Add the fraction part of the mixed number first. Then add the whole numbers.

$\frac{9}{12} + \frac{10}{12} = \frac{19}{12}$     $3 + 2 = 5$

$\frac{19}{12} + 5 = 5\frac{19}{12}$

**Step 3.** Simplify the sum if possible.

$5\frac{19}{12} = 6\frac{7}{12}$ hours

So, $2\frac{5}{6} + 3\frac{3}{4} = 6\frac{7}{12}$.

In **1** through **6**, find each sum. Simplify if possible.

**1.**  $2\frac{10}{12}$
    $+ 3\frac{3}{12}$
    _____

**2.**  $1\frac{3}{8}$
    $+ 6\frac{6}{8}$
    _____

**3.**  $5\frac{4}{10}$
    $+ 4\frac{2}{10}$
    _____

**4.** $10\frac{2}{6} + \frac{3}{6} =$ _____

**5.** $3\frac{3}{12} + 6\frac{8}{12} =$ _____

**6.** $1\frac{2}{5} + 3\frac{1}{5} =$ _____

**7. Geometry** Tirzah wants to put a fence around her garden. She has 22 yards of fence material. Does she have enough to go all the way around the garden?

_____

_____

_____

_____

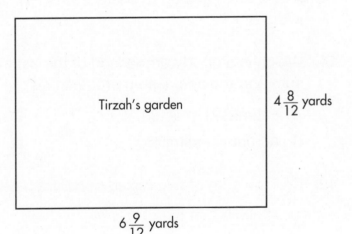

Tirzah's garden

$4\frac{8}{12}$ yards

$6\frac{9}{12}$ yards

Name _____

# Adding Mixed Numbers

In **1** through **6**, find each sum. Simplify, if possible. Estimate for reasonableness.

1. $7\frac{2}{6} + 8\frac{5}{6}$ _____

2. $4\frac{3}{4} + 2\frac{2}{4}$ _____

3. $11\frac{9}{10} + 3\frac{2}{10}$ _____

4. $7\frac{9}{8} + 5\frac{2}{8}$ _____

5. $5\frac{8}{12} + 3\frac{5}{12}$ _____

6. $21\frac{11}{12} + 17\frac{5}{12}$ _____

7. **Number Sense** Write two mixed numbers that have a sum of 3.

_____

8. What is the total measure of an average man's brain and heart in kilograms (kg)?

_____

**Vital Organ Measures**

| | | |
|---|---|---|
| Average woman's brain | $1\frac{3}{10}$ kg | $2\frac{8}{10}$ lb |
| Average man's brain | $1\frac{4}{10}$ kg | 3 lb |
| Average human heart | $\frac{3}{10}$ kg | $\frac{7}{10}$ lb |

9. What is the total weight of an average woman's brain and heart in pounds (lb)?

_____

10. What is the sum of the measures of an average man's brain and an average woman's brain in kilograms?

_____

11. Which is a good comparison of the estimated sum and the actual sum of $7\frac{9}{12} + 2\frac{11}{12}$?

**A** Estimated < actual

**B** Actual = estimated

**C** Actual > estimated

**D** Estimated > actual

12. Can the sum of two mixed numbers be equal to 2? Explain why or why not.

_____

_____

_____

# Subtracting Mixed Numbers

The Plainville Zoo has had elephants for $12\frac{4}{6}$ years. The zoo has had zebras for $5\frac{3}{6}$ years. How many years longer has the zoo had elephants?

**Step 1:** Write equivalent fractions with the least common denominator. You can use fraction strips.

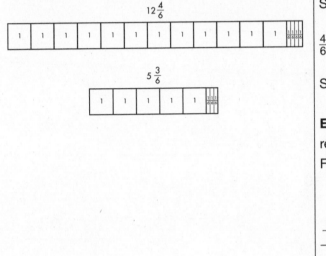

**Step 2:** Find the difference of $12\frac{4}{6} - 5\frac{3}{6}$. Subtract the fractions. Then subtract the whole numbers. Simplify the difference if possible.

$\frac{4}{6} - \frac{3}{6} = \frac{1}{6}$           $12 - 5 = 7$

So, $12\frac{4}{6} - 5\frac{3}{6} = 7\frac{1}{6}$ years.

**Example 2:** Sometimes you may have to rename a fraction so you can subtract. Find the difference of $6 - 2\frac{3}{8}$.

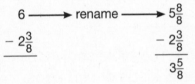

For **1** through **4**, find each difference. Simplify, if possible.
Remember: You may have to rename a fraction in order to subtract.

1.  $4\frac{5}{8}$
   $-2\frac{2}{8}$

2.  $5\frac{7}{12}$
   $-1\frac{2}{12}$

3.  $3$
   $-1\frac{3}{4}$

4.  $6\frac{5}{6}$
   $-5\frac{4}{6}$

5.  **Number Sense** To find the difference of $7 - 3\frac{5}{12}$, how do you rename the 7?

_____

6.  Robyn ran $5\frac{3}{4}$ miles last week. She ran $4\frac{1}{4}$ miles this week. How many more miles did she run last week?

_____

Name _____

# Subtracting Mixed Numbers

For **1** through **10**, find each difference. Simplify, if possible.

1. $10\frac{3}{4}$
$- 7\frac{1}{4}$
_____

2. $7\frac{4}{6}$
$- 2\frac{3}{6}$
_____

3. $3$
$- 2\frac{2}{3}$
_____

4. $17\frac{8}{12}$
$- 12\frac{3}{12}$
_____

5. $9\frac{2}{6} - 6\frac{5}{6}$ _____

6. $4\frac{1}{5} - 2\frac{3}{5}$ _____

7. $6\frac{3}{12} - 3\frac{4}{12}$ _____

8. $5\frac{2}{8} - 3\frac{7}{8}$ _____

9. $8\frac{1}{4} - 7\frac{3}{4}$ _____

10. $2\frac{9}{10} - 2\frac{5}{10}$ _____

**Strategy Practice** The table shows the length
and width of several kinds of bird eggs.

11. How much longer is the Canada
goose egg than the raven egg?

_____

12. How much wider is the turtledove
egg than the robin egg?

_____

### Egg Sizes in Inches (in.)

| Bird | Length | Width |
|------|--------|-------|
| Canada goose | $3\frac{4}{10}$ | $2\frac{3}{10}$ |
| Robin | $\frac{8}{10}$ | $\frac{6}{10}$ |
| Turtledove | $1\frac{2}{10}$ | $\frac{9}{10}$ |
| Raven | $1\frac{9}{10}$ | $1\frac{3}{10}$ |

13. Which is the difference of $21\frac{1}{4} - 18\frac{2}{4}$?

A $2\frac{1}{4}$     B $2\frac{2}{4}$     C $2\frac{3}{4}$     D $3\frac{1}{4}$

14. Explain why it is necessary to rename $4\frac{1}{4}$ if you subtract $\frac{3}{4}$ from it.

_____

_____

# Decomposing and Composing Fractions

**Example 1**

$\begin{array}{r} \frac{1}{9} \\ + \ \frac{2}{9} \\ \hline \end{array}$

The denominators are the same, so you can add the numerators.

$\frac{3}{9} = \frac{1}{3}$  Rewrite $\frac{3}{9}$ as $\frac{1}{3}$

**Example 2**

$\frac{1}{8} + \frac{3}{8} + \frac{5}{8} = \frac{9}{8}$ or $1\frac{1}{8}$

Show another way to make this sum.

$\frac{6}{8} + \frac{3}{8} = \frac{9}{8} = 1\frac{1}{8}$

Add or subtract fractions and write answers in simplest form.
For the addition problems, write another addition problem that
has the same sum and uses two or more fractions.

**1.** $\frac{1}{4} + \frac{1}{4}$     **2.** $\frac{2}{3} - \frac{1}{3}$     **3.** $\frac{2}{8} + \frac{5}{8}$     **4.** $\frac{5}{6} - \frac{1}{6}$     **5.** $\frac{4}{12} + \frac{2}{12}$

_____   _____   _____   _____   _____

**6.** $\begin{array}{r} \frac{5}{6} \\ - \ \frac{2}{6} \\ \hline \end{array}$     **7.** $\begin{array}{r} \frac{3}{10} \\ + \ \frac{3}{10} \\ \hline \end{array}$     **8.** $\begin{array}{r} \frac{9}{10} \\ - \ \frac{3}{10} \\ \hline \end{array}$     **9.** $\begin{array}{r} \frac{3}{12} \\ + \ \frac{6}{12} \\ \hline \end{array}$     **10.** $\begin{array}{r} \frac{44}{100} \\ - \ \frac{24}{100} \\ \hline \end{array}$

**11.** At lunch, Alice ate $\frac{3}{8}$ of her sandwich. Later, for a snack, she ate another $\frac{3}{8}$ of the sandwich. Write an addition sentence that shows how much of the sandwich Alice ate. Suppose Alice ate the same total amount of her sandwich at 3 different times instead of 2. Write an addition problem that shows the amount she ate as a sum of 3 fractions.

_____

_____

# Decomposing and Composing Fractions

For **1** through **15**, add or subtract the fractions. For the addition problems, write another addition problem that has the same sum and uses two or more fractions.

**1.** $\frac{1}{8} + \frac{3}{8} =$ _____

**2.** $\frac{8}{10} + \frac{1}{10} =$ _____

**3.** $\frac{1}{3} + \frac{1}{3} =$ _____

**4.** $\frac{3}{8}$
$+ \frac{3}{8}$
_____

**5.** $\frac{1}{5}$
$+ \frac{2}{5}$
_____

**6.** $\frac{3}{6}$
$+ \frac{2}{6}$
_____

**7.** $\frac{9}{12} - \frac{2}{12} =$ _____

**8.** $\frac{4}{8} - \frac{2}{8} =$ _____

**9.** $\frac{6}{10} - \frac{1}{10} =$ _____

**10.** $\frac{5}{8}$
$- \frac{2}{8}$
_____

**11.** $\frac{7}{10}$
$- \frac{1}{10}$
_____

**12.** $\frac{8}{10}$
$- \frac{4}{10}$
_____

**13.** $\frac{1}{6}$
$+ \frac{2}{6}$
_____

**14.** $\frac{1}{3}$
$+ \frac{1}{3}$
_____

**15.** $\frac{1}{4}$
$+ \frac{1}{4}$
_____

**16.** Jacob is making a stew. The stew calls for $\frac{3}{8}$ cup of rice. If he triples the recipe, how much rice will he need? Write an addition problem to show your answer.

_____

**17.** Which of the following fractions is not an equivalent fraction to $\frac{1}{2}$?

**A** $\frac{3}{6}$     **B** $\frac{4}{8}$     **C** $\frac{6}{10}$     **D** $\frac{6}{12}$

**18.** **Writing to Explain** Gerry folded $\frac{3}{8}$ of the pile of shirts. Molly folded $\frac{1}{8}$ of the pile of shirts. Together, did they fold more than half the shirts? Explain your answer.

_____

# Problem Solving: Draw a Picture and Write an Equation

**Read and Understand**    Pippa filled $\frac{1}{8}$ of a jar with blue stones, $\frac{2}{8}$ of the jar with yellow stones, and $\frac{4}{8}$ of the jar with purple stones. How much of the jar is filled in all?

What do I know?    Pippa filled $\frac{1}{8}$, $\frac{2}{8}$, and $\frac{4}{8}$ of a jar.

What am I asked to find?    How much of the jar is filled with stones?

**Plan**    Draw a picture and write an equation.

| x | | |
|---|---|---|
| $\frac{1}{8}$ | $\frac{2}{8}$ | $\frac{4}{8}$ |

$\frac{1}{8} + \frac{2}{8} + \frac{4}{8} = x$

**Solve**    Find equal fractions and add. Simplify if you need to.

$\frac{1}{8} + \frac{2}{8} + \frac{4}{8} = \frac{7}{8}$

$x = \frac{7}{8}$

Pippa filled the jar $\frac{7}{8}$ full of stones.

Draw a picture and write an equation to solve.

1. Joel walked $\frac{4}{12}$ of a mile to the store, $\frac{3}{12}$ of a mile to the library, and $\frac{2}{12}$ of a mile to the post office. Let $x$ = the total distance Joel walked. How far did he walk?

_____

2. Midge walked $\frac{3}{4}$ mile Monday and $\frac{1}{4}$ mile Tuesday. Let $x$ = how much farther she walked on Monday. How much farther did Midge walk on Monday?

_____

3. **Number Sense** Glenda wrote $\frac{2}{10}$ of her paper on Monday, $\frac{1}{10}$ of her paper on Tuesday, and $\frac{1}{10}$ of her paper on Wednesday. She said she wrote more than half of her paper. Is she correct? Why or why not?

_____

_____

# Problem Solving: Draw a Picture and Write an Equation

Draw a picture and write an equation to solve.

1. Jamie bought $\frac{5}{8}$ pound of wheat flour. He also bought $\frac{2}{8}$ pound of white flour. How much flour did he buy?

2. Katie is $\frac{6}{10}$ of the way to Brianna's house. Larry is $\frac{7}{10}$ of the way to Brianna's house. How much closer to Brianna's house is Larry?

3. Nina practiced the trumpet for $\frac{1}{6}$ hour. Santiago practiced the trumpet for $\frac{4}{6}$ hour. How much longer did Santiago practice than Nina?

4. Ned caught $\frac{4}{12}$ pound of fish. Sarah caught $\frac{5}{12}$ pound of fish. Jessa caught $\frac{6}{12}$ pound of fish. Which bar diagram shows how to find how many pounds of fish they caught in all?

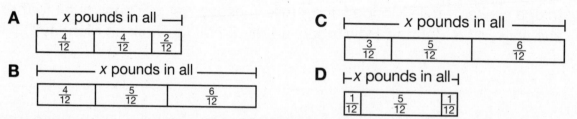

5. John had $\frac{5}{8}$ of a pizza left after a party. He gave $\frac{3}{8}$ of the pizza to his friend to take home and he kept the rest. Draw a picture showing what fraction of the pizza John kept, and write an equation to solve.

_____

_____

# Fractions as Multiples of Unit Fractions: Using Models

Ricardo has an apple that is cut into quarters.

He wants to eat $\frac{3}{4}$ of the apple.

How many $\frac{1}{4}$ pieces does he need to make $\frac{3}{4}$?

Use fraction strips and a number line.

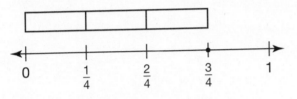

Each fraction strip equals $\frac{1}{4}$.

There are three $\frac{1}{4}$ fraction strips.

$$\frac{3}{4} = 3 \times \frac{1}{4}$$

Ricardo needs three $\frac{1}{4}$ pieces to make $\frac{3}{4}$.

In **1** and **2**, use the number line and fraction strips to complete the equation.

**1.**

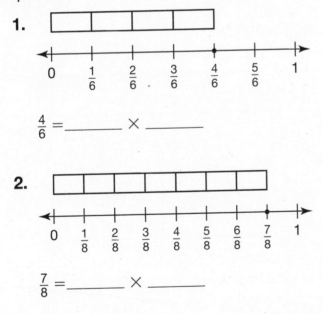

$\frac{4}{6} =$ _____ $\times$ _____

**2.**

$\frac{7}{8} =$ _____ $\times$ _____

# Fractions as Multiples of Unit Fractions: Using Models

For **1** through **9**, write the fraction as a multiple of a unit fraction. Use fraction strips to help.

**1.** $\frac{2}{4} =$ _____

**2.** $\frac{4}{6} =$ _____

**3.** $\frac{3}{5} =$ _____

**4.** $\frac{3}{3} =$ _____

**5.** $\frac{7}{8} =$ _____

**6.** $\frac{6}{2} =$ _____

**7.** $\frac{5}{6} =$ _____

**8.** $\frac{9}{5} =$ _____

**9.** $\frac{8}{3} =$ _____

**10.** Use the picture at the right to write a multiplication equation with $\frac{1}{2}$ as a factor. Explain how you found the answer.

_____

_____

_____

**11.** How can you tell that a fraction is a unit fraction?

_____

_____

**12.** Which equation describes the picture?

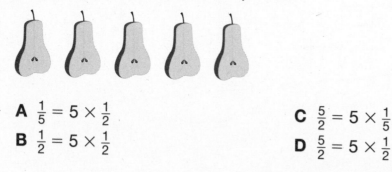

**A** $\frac{1}{5} = 5 \times \frac{1}{2}$

**B** $\frac{1}{2} = 5 \times \frac{1}{2}$

**C** $\frac{5}{2} = 5 \times \frac{1}{5}$

**D** $\frac{5}{2} = 5 \times \frac{1}{2}$

# Multiplying a Fraction by a Whole Number: Using Models

Write a multiplication equation of a whole number times a fraction to go with the picture.

| $\frac{1}{5}$ | $\frac{1}{5}$ | $\frac{1}{5}$ | $\frac{1}{5}$ | $\frac{1}{5}$ | $\frac{1}{5}$ |
|---|---|---|---|---|---|

Find the unit fraction: $\frac{1}{5}$

Count the number of unit fractions: 6

Write a multiplication equation to show the number of unit fractions times the unit fraction. $6 \times \frac{1}{5} =$ ▉

Multiply to find the product. $6 \times \frac{1}{5} = \frac{6}{5}$

The multiplication equation that goes with the picture is $6 \times \frac{1}{5} = \frac{6}{5}$.

In **1–2**, write a multiplication equation of a whole number and a fraction to go with the picture.

**1.**

| $\frac{1}{3}$ | $\frac{1}{3}$ | $\frac{1}{3}$ | $\frac{1}{3}$ | $\frac{1}{3}$ | $\frac{1}{3}$ | $\frac{1}{3}$ | $\frac{1}{3}$ |
|---|---|---|---|---|---|---|---|

Unit fraction: _____

Number of unit fractions: _____

Multiplication equation: _____

**2.**

| $\frac{1}{4}$ | $\frac{1}{4}$ | $\frac{1}{4}$ | $\frac{1}{4}$ | $\frac{1}{4}$ | $\frac{1}{4}$ | $\frac{1}{4}$ | $\frac{1}{4}$ | $\frac{1}{4}$ |
|---|---|---|---|---|---|---|---|---|

Unit fraction: _____

Number of unit fractions: _____

Multiplication equation: _____

# Multiplying a Fraction by a Whole Number: Using Models

For **1–3**, use each model to write a multiplication equation with a whole number and a fraction.

**1.**

| $\frac{1}{6}$ | $\frac{1}{6}$ | $\frac{1}{6}$ | $\frac{1}{6}$ | $\frac{1}{6}$ | $\frac{1}{6}$ | $\frac{1}{6}$ | $\frac{1}{6}$ | $\frac{1}{6}$ | $\frac{1}{6}$ |

$\frac{5}{6}$     $\frac{5}{6}$

_____

**2.**

| $\frac{4}{12}$ | $\frac{4}{12}$ | $\frac{4}{12}$ | $\frac{4}{12}$ | $\frac{4}{12}$ |

_____

**3.**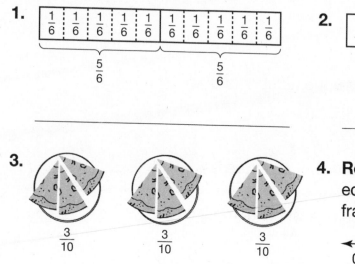

$\frac{3}{10}$     $\frac{3}{10}$     $\frac{3}{10}$

_____

**4. Reason** Write a multiplication equation of a whole number times a fraction to go with the number line.

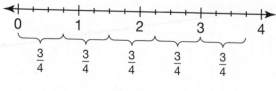

$\frac{3}{4}$   $\frac{3}{4}$   $\frac{3}{4}$   $\frac{3}{4}$   $\frac{3}{4}$

_____

**5. Model** Explain why $4 \times \frac{3}{5} = \frac{(4 \times 3)}{5} = \frac{12}{5}$. Draw a picture.

_____

**6.** Audrey uses $\frac{5}{8}$ cup of fruit in each smoothie she makes. She makes 6 smoothies to share with her friends. How many cups of fruit does she use?

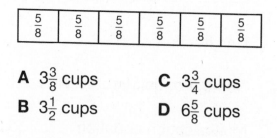

**A** $3\frac{3}{8}$ cups     **C** $3\frac{3}{4}$ cups

**B** $3\frac{1}{2}$ cups     **D** $6\frac{5}{8}$ cups

# Multiplying a Fraction by a Whole Number: Using Symbols

Josh has 4 pieces of rope. Each piece of rope is $\frac{3}{4}$ yard long. How many yards of rope does Josh have?

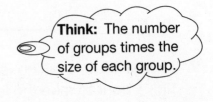

You can think of each piece of rope as a separate group. The size of each group is $\frac{3}{4}$ yard.

$$\frac{3}{4} + \frac{3}{4} + \frac{3}{4} + \frac{3}{4}$$

Since all of the groups are the same size, you can use multiplication to find the total.

$$4 \times \frac{3}{4} = \frac{(4 \times 3)}{4} = \frac{12}{4} = 3$$

**Think:** The number of groups times the size of each group.

Josh has 3 yards of rope.

Solve. Show your work.

1. Mia is painting her room. Her room has 4 walls. Each wall uses $\frac{2}{3}$ gallon of paint. How much paint does she need to paint all of her walls?

   $$\frac{2}{3} + \frac{2}{3} + \frac{2}{3} + \frac{2}{3} = 4 \times \frac{2}{3}$$

   $4 \times \frac{2}{3} =$ _____

2. Nat has 5 pieces of string. Each piece is $\frac{7}{8}$ inch long. How many inches of string does Nat have?

   $$\frac{7}{8} + \frac{7}{8} + \frac{7}{8} + \frac{7}{8} + \frac{7}{8} = 5 \times \frac{7}{8}$$

   $5 \times \frac{7}{8} =$ _____

3. Caroline is making 8 batches of biscuits. Each batch uses $\frac{5}{6}$ cup of flour. How many cups of flour does Caroline need?

   _____

   _____

Name _____

# Multiplying a Fraction by a Whole Number: Using Symbols

For **1–8**, multiply.

1. $8 \times \frac{5}{12} =$ _____

2. $9 \times \frac{1}{4} =$ _____

3. $5 \times \frac{3}{5} =$ _____

4. $10 \times \frac{5}{6} =$ _____

5. $9 \times \frac{3}{10} =$ _____

6. $7 \times \frac{1}{3} =$ _____

7. $12 \times \frac{1}{5} =$ _____

8. $11 \times \frac{7}{8} =$ _____

9. **Model** Matt is raking leaves for his neighbors. It takes him $\frac{7}{8}$ hour to rake the leaves in one lawn. How long will it take Matt to rake the leaves for 6 neighbors? Write a multiplication sentence to solve.

_____

10. Zoey is making bracelets for her friends. Each bracelet takes $\frac{5}{6}$ foot of string. How much string will Zoey need to make 12 bracelets?

_____

11. Farid takes $\frac{7}{8}$ teaspoon of allergy medicine every day. How much medicine will he take in one week?

**A** $1\frac{3}{4}$ teaspoons   **B** $5\frac{1}{4}$ teaspoons   **C** $6\frac{1}{8}$ teaspoons   **D** $7\frac{7}{8}$ teaspoons

12. **Writing to Explain** Mrs. Nunez is correcting math tests. She corrects 7 tests before school, and 5 tests after school. If each test takes her $\frac{1}{5}$ hour to correct, how long will it take Mrs. Nunez to correct the tests? Explain.

_____

_____

_____

# Fractions and Decimals

Any fraction that has a denominator of 10 or 100 can be written as a decimal. Tenths and hundredths are written as digits to the right of the decimal point.

The shaded part is $\frac{2}{10}$ of the whole area.

Write it as a decimal: 0.2

Say: two tenths.

The shaded part is $\frac{13}{100}$ of the whole area.

Write it as a decimal: 0.13

Say: thirteen hundredths

---

Write a fraction and a decimal to tell how much is shaded.

**1.** 

_____

**2.** 

_____

**3.** How are the two shaded grids alike? How are they different?

_____

_____

_____

_____

Write each fraction as a decimal.

**4.** $\frac{3}{10}$

_____

**5.** $\frac{9}{10}$

_____

**6.** $\frac{9}{100}$

_____

**7.** $\frac{27}{100}$

_____

Write each decimal as a fraction in its simplest form.

**8.** 0.40

**9.** 0.76

**10.** 4.8

**11.** 0.07

_____

# Fractions and Decimals

Write a fraction and a decimal to show how much is shaded.

**1.**

_____

**2.**

_____

**3.**

_____

Draw a model that shows each decimal.

**4.** 0.16

**5.** 1.7

**6.** 0.78

Write each fraction as a decimal.

**7.** $\frac{1}{100}$

_____

**8.** $9\frac{4}{10}$

_____

**9.** $\frac{6}{10}$

_____

**10.** $\frac{17}{100}$

_____

Write each decimal as a fraction in its simplest form.

**11.** 0.5

_____

**12.** 0.70

_____

**13.** 0.3

_____

**14.** 3.60

_____

**15.** In the decimal models, how many strips equal 10 small squares?

**A** 70 strips  **B** 10 strips  **C** 7 strips  **D** 1 strip

**16. Writing to Explain** Explain the steps you would take to write $\frac{36}{10}$ as a decimal.

_____

_____

_____

# Fractions and Decimals on the Number Line

How do you locate fractions and decimals on a number line?

Show $\frac{1}{8}$ on a number line.

Draw a number line and label 0 and 1. Divide the distance from 0 to 1 into 8 equal lengths.

Label 0, $\frac{1}{8}$, $\frac{2}{8}$, $\frac{3}{8}$, $\frac{4}{8}$, $\frac{5}{8}$, $\frac{6}{8}$, $\frac{7}{8}$, and 1.

Draw a point at $\frac{1}{8}$.

Show 0.3 on another number line.

Draw another number line and label 0 and 1. Divide the distance from 0 to 1 into 10 equal lengths.

Label 0.1, 0.2, 0.3, 0.4, and so on.

8 equal parts

1 out of 8 equal parts

10 equal parts

3 out of 10 equal parts

Use the number line to name the fraction that should be written at each point.

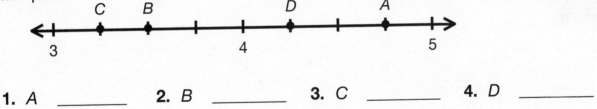

**1.** A _____  **2.** B _____  **3.** C _____  **4.** D _____

Identify the correct point on the number line for each fraction or decimal.

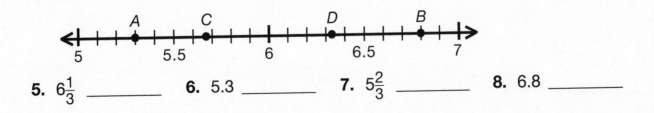

**5.** $6\frac{1}{3}$ _____  **6.** 5.3 _____  **7.** $5\frac{2}{3}$ _____  **8.** 6.8 _____

# Fractions and Decimals on the Number Line

Use the number line to name the fraction or decimal that should be written at each point.

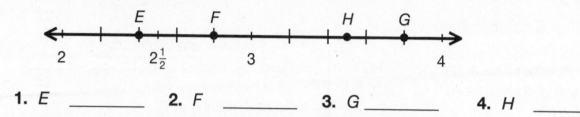

1. E _____
2. F _____
3. G _____
4. H _____

Identify the correct point on the number line for each fraction or decimal.

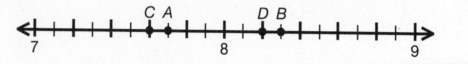

5. 8.3 _____
6. $7\frac{3}{5}$ _____
7. 7.7 _____
8. 8.2 _____

9. Eamon used a number line to compare two numbers, 0.48 and $\frac{3}{5}$. One number was less than $\frac{1}{2}$ and the other number was greater than $\frac{1}{2}$. Which number was less than $\frac{1}{2}$? _____

10. **Writing to Explain** Jayne says that 0.45 is equal to $\frac{4}{10}$. Is she correct? Explain.

_____

_____

_____

Name _____

# Equivalent Fractions and Decimals

A fraction and a decimal can both be used to represent the same value.

Write $\frac{6}{12}$ as a decimal.

**Step 1**  Write the fraction in simplest form.

$$\frac{6}{12} = \frac{1}{2}$$

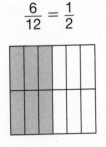

**Step 2**  Rename the fraction using a denominator of 10, 100, or 1,000.

Think: What number times 2 equals 10?

$$\frac{1}{2} \overset{\times 5}{\underset{\times 5}{=}} \frac{5}{10}$$

**Step 3**  Write the decimal.

$\frac{5}{10}$ is five tenths.

$$\frac{5}{10} = 0.5$$

So, $\frac{6}{12} = 0.5$

In **1** through **4**, find the missing numbers. Then write each fraction as a decimal.

**1.** $\frac{1}{4} = \frac{\square}{100}$

**2.** $\frac{9}{20} = \frac{\square}{100}$

**3.** $\frac{3}{15} = \frac{1}{\square} = \frac{\square}{10}$

**4.** $\frac{8}{25} = \frac{\square}{100}$

_____     _____     _____     _____

Write each fraction as a decimal.

**5.** $\frac{4}{5}$

**6.** $\frac{4}{50}$

**7.** $\frac{4}{25}$

**8.** $\frac{13}{20}$

**9.** $\frac{9}{50}$

_____     _____     _____     _____     _____

Tell whether each pair shows equivalent numbers.

**10.** $\frac{2}{5}$; 0.25     **11.** $\frac{10}{25}$; 0.4     **12.** $\frac{3}{5}$; 0.35     **13.** $\frac{7}{20}$; 0.35

_____     _____     _____     _____

**14.** Nine out of 15, or $\frac{9}{15}$, of the people at the skating rink brought their own skates. Write an equivalent decimal for $\frac{9}{15}$. _____

Name _____

# Equivalent Fractions and Decimals

In **1** through **5**, write each fraction as a decimal.

**1.** $\frac{1}{5}$　　　**2.** $\frac{9}{12}$　　　**3.** $\frac{11}{25}$　　　**4.** $\frac{19}{20}$　　　**5.** $\frac{23}{50}$

_____　　_____　　_____　　_____　　_____

In **6** through **9**, tell whether each pair shows equivalent numbers.

**6.** $\frac{2}{5}$; 0.5　　　**7.** $\frac{7}{20}$; 0.07　　　**8.** $\frac{4}{16}$; 0.25　　　**9.** $\frac{11}{50}$; 0.22

_____　　　_____　　　　_____　　　_____

**10.** A rock band has 5 members, and $\frac{2}{5}$ of the members play string instruments. Also, 0.4 of the members sing. Does the band have the same number of string instrument players as singers? Explain.

**11.** Kevin has 20 words to learn for his spelling test on Friday. He has learned 6 of the words. So, he has learned $\frac{6}{20}$ of the words. Write $\frac{6}{20}$ in simplest form, and find an equivalent decimal.

_____

**12.** Which decimal is equivalent to $\frac{5}{20}$?

**A** 0.20　　　**C** 0.35

**B** 0.25　　　**D** 0.52

**13.** Gina wrote that $\frac{4}{5}$ is greater than 0.75. Is Gina correct? Explain why or why not.

_____

**14.** Look at Exercise 8. Explain how you decided whether the numbers are equivalent.

_____

_____

# Decimal Place Value

A grid can be used to show tenths and hundredths. To show 0.3, you would shade 3 out of the 10 parts.

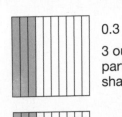

0.3
3 out of 10 parts are shaded.

To show 0.30, you would shade 30 out of the 100 parts.

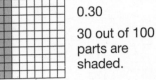

0.30
30 out of 100 parts are shaded.

One part of the hundredths grid can be compared to a penny, since one part of the grid is equal to 0.01 and a penny is equal to one hundredth of a dollar.

Tenths and hundredths are related. In the above examples, 3 tenths or 30 hundredths of the grids are shaded, or 0.3 and 0.30. These numbers are equal: 0.3 = 0.30.

Write the word form and decimal for each shaded part.

**1.**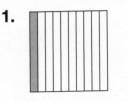

_____

**2.**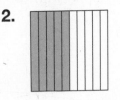

_____

Shade each grid to show the decimal.

**3.** 0.57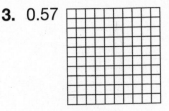

**4.** 0.4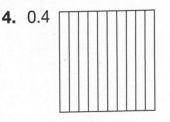

**5. Number Sense** Which is greater, 0.04 or 0.4? Explain.

_____

_____

_____

_____

# Decimal Place Value

Write the word form and decimal for each shaded part.

**1.**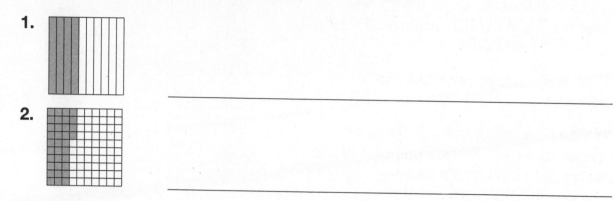

_____

**2.**

_____

For each fact, shade a grid to show the part of the population of each country that lives in cities.

**3.** In Jamaica, 0.5 of the people live in cities.

**4.** Only 0.11 of the population of Uganda live in cities.

**5.** In Norway, 0.72 of the people live in cities.

**6.** Which grid shows fourteen hundredths?

A          B          C          D

**7.** **Writing to Explain** Explain why one column in a hundredths grid is equal to one column in a tenths grid.

_____

_____

_____

# Comparing and Ordering Decimals

Compare 0.87 to 0.89.

First, begin at the left. Find the first place where the numbers are different.

0.87

0.89

The numbers are the same in the tenths place, so look to the next place.

The first place where the numbers are different is the hundredths place. Compare 7 hundredths to 9 hundredths.

0.07 < 0.09, so 0.87 < 0.89

Compare. Write >, <, or = for each ◯.

**1.** 0.36 ◯ 0.76

**2.** 5.1 ◯ 5.01

**3.** 1.2 ◯ 1.20

**4.** 6.55 ◯ 6.6

**5.** 0.62 ◯ 0.82

**6.** 4.71 ◯ 4.17

Order the numbers from least to greatest.

**7.** 1.36, 1.3, 1.63

**8.** 0.42, 3.74, 3.47

_____

_____

**9.** 6.46, 6.41, 4.6

**10.** 0.3, 0.13, 0.19, 0.31

_____

_____

**11. Number Sense** Which is greater, 8.0 or 0.8? Explain.

_____

_____

_____

Name _____

# Comparing and Ordering Decimals

Compare. Write >, <, or = for each ◯.

**1.** 0.31 ◯ 0.41

**2.** 1.9 ◯ 0.95

**3.** 0.09 ◯ 0.1

**4.** 2.70 ◯ 2.7

**5.** 0.81 ◯ 0.79

**6.** 2.12 ◯ 2.21

Order the numbers from least to greatest.

**7.** 0.37, 0.41, 0.31

**8.** 1.16, 1.61, 6.11

_____

_____

**9.** 7.9, 7.91, 7.09, 7.19

**10.** 1.45, 1.76, 1.47, 1.67

_____

_____

Margaret has three cats. Sophie weighs 4.27 lb, Tigger weighs 6.25 lb, and Ghost weighs 4.7 lb.

**11.** Which cat has the greatest weight? _____

**12.** Which cat weighs the least? _____

**13.** Which group of numbers is ordered from least to greatest?

    **A** 0.12, 1.51, 0.65

    **B** 5.71, 5.4, 0.54

    **C** 0.4, 0.09, 0.41

    **D** 0.05, 0.51, 1.5

**14.** **Writing to Explain** Darrin put the numbers 7.25, 7.52, 5.72, and 5.27 in order from greatest to least. Is his work correct? Explain.

_____

_____

Name _____

# Using Money
# to Understand Decimals

We can use money to understand decimals. For example, a dime
is one-tenth of a dollar, or 0.1. It takes 10 dimes to equal a dollar.
A penny is one one-hundredth of a dollar, or 0.01, so it takes
100 pennies to equal one dollar.

| $0.01 | $0.05 | $0.10 | $0.25 | $0.50 |
|-------|-------|-------|-------|-------|
| 0.01  | 0.05  | 0.1   | 0.25  | 0.5   |

The decimal point is read by saying "and." So, $1.99 is read as
"one dollar *and* ninety-nine cents."

1. $3.52 = _____ dollars + _____ dimes + _____ pennies

2. $1.87 = _____ dollar + _____ dimes + _____ pennies

3. **Number Sense** Write nine and thirty-six hundredths
   with a decimal point. _____

How could you use only dollars,
dimes, and pennies to buy

4. the baseball?

   _____

   _____

5. the baseball bat?

   _____

   _____

$3.99

$8.49

$12.20

Name _____

# Using Money to Understand Decimals

**1.** 2.18 = _____ ones + _____ tenth + _____ hundredths

$2.18 = _____ dollars + _____ dime + _____ pennies

**2.** 9.27 = _____ ones + _____ hundredths

$9.27 = _____ dollars + _____ pennies

**3.** 7.39 = _____ ones + _____ tenths + _____ hundredths

$7.39 = _____ dollars + _____ dimes + _____ pennies

**4. Number Sense** Write 3 dollars, 9 dimes, and 5 pennies with a dollar sign and decimal point.

_____

**5. Number Sense** If you have 5 tenths of a dollar, how much money do you have?

_____

**6.** Lana wants to buy a book for $6.95. How can she pay for the book using only dollars, dimes, and nickels?

_____

**7.** How would you write sixteen and twenty-five hundredths with a decimal point?

**A** 16.025      **B** 16.25      **C** 162.5      **D** 1,625

**8. Writing to Explain** Which is greater, 4 tenths and 2 hundredths or 2 tenths and 4 hundredths? Explain.

_____

_____

_____

Name _____

# Problem Solving:
# Draw a Picture

A fence is 20 ft long. It has posts at each end and at every 4 ft along its length. How many fence posts are there?

### Read and Understand

**Step 1: What do you know?**

The fence is 20 ft long.

There are fence posts at each end.

There are fence posts every 4 ft along the length of the fence.

**Step 2: What are you trying to find?**

How many posts the fence has.

### Plan and Solve

**Step 3: What strategy will you use?**

**Strategy:** Draw a picture

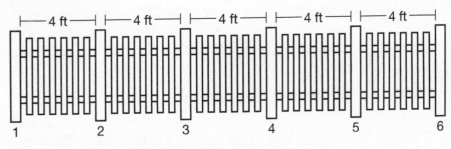

There are 6 fence posts altogether.

### Look Back and Check

**Step 4: Is your work correct?**

Yes, the picture shows that there is a total of 6 fence posts.

Solve the problem. Write the answer in a complete sentence.

1. Tim, Kara, and Ann are working together to write a 4-page report. Each student is going to do an equal amount of writing. What fraction of the entire report does each student need to write?

Name _____

# Problem Solving:
# Draw a Picture

Solve each problem. Write the answer in a complete sentence.

1. Three friends divided a veggie pizza into 12 slices. If they divide the pizza equally, what fraction of the pizza would each friend get?

   _____

2. Mark is making a quilt with his grandmother. Each row of the quilt has 6 squares. There are 8 rows. $\frac{1}{2}$ of the squares are blue. How many blue squares are in the quilt?

   _____

3. Jane pulled weeds in the garden 7 times. She was paid $5 each time she pulled weeds for less than 1 hour and $6 each time she pulled weeds for more than 1 hour. If Jane received $39, how many times did she pull weeds for more than 1 hour?

   _____

   _____

4. Neil needs to cut 3 long boards into 9 smaller boards. The first is 10 ft, the second is 16 ft, and the third is 18 ft. The table lists the smaller boards Neil needs. Use a drawing to show how he can divide the 3 boards so there is no waste.

| Length of Board | Number Needed |
|---|---|
| 4 ft | 3 |
| 5 ft | 4 |
| 6 ft | 2 |

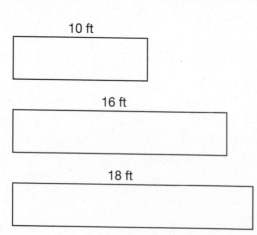

10 ft

16 ft

18 ft

Name _____

# Customary Units of Length

| Unit | Example |
|------|---------|
| inch | width of a U.S. quarter |
| 1 foot (ft) = 12 inches (in.) | gym shoes |
| 1 yard (yd) = 3 feet | height of a desk |
| 1 mile (mi) = 5,280 feet | distance between school and home |

**How to measure an object:**

To measure an object, make sure one end of the object begins at the zero unit.

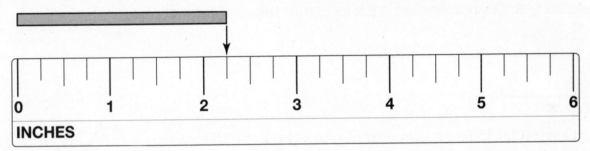

The rectangle is closest to the 2 in. mark, so we can say the rectangle is 2 in. long to the nearest inch.

Choose the most appropriate unit to measure the length of each.
Write in., ft, yd, or mi.

**1.** cat _____

**2.** lake _____

**3.** hallway _____

**4.** basketball court _____

Estimate first. Then, find each length to the nearest inch.

**5.** ⊢————————————————⊣ _____

**6.** ⊢————⊣ _____

# Customary Units of Length

Choose the most appropriate unit to measure the length of each. Write in., ft, yd, or mi.

1. boat _____    2. wallet _____

3. soccer field _____    4. finger bandage _____

5. computer cable _____    6. train route _____

7. nose _____    8. sea _____

Estimate first. Then, measure each length to the nearest inch.

9. |———————————————|    _____

10. |—————————|    _____

11. Use a ruler to find the length of one side of the triangle. Then find the perimeter.

_____

12. Eileen needs 9 feet of fabric to make a skirt. If Eileen has 18 feet of fabric how many skirts can she make?

_____

13. Which unit would be most appropriate for measuring the length of a barn?

   A inches        B pounds        C yards        D miles

14. **Writing to Explain** Explain how you would decide which unit is best for measuring your math book.

_____

_____

Name _____

# Customary Units of Capacity

Capacity is the amount that a container can hold. Capacity is measured in teaspoons, tablespoons, fluid ounces, cups, pints, quarts, and gallons, from smallest to largest.

a cup

There are 2 cups in a pint.

There are 2 pints in a quart.

There are 4 quarts in a gallon.

Choose the most appropriate unit or units to measure the capacity of each. Write fl oz, c, pt, qt, or gal.

1. water bottle _____

2. bathtub _____

3. milk carton _____

4. coffee pot _____

5. teacup _____

6. jug of juice _____

7. **Reasoning** Would a cup be a good tool for measuring the amount of water in a bathtub? Explain why or why not.

_____

_____

The adult human body contains about 5 qt of blood.

8. Are there more or less than 5 pt of blood in a human adult?

9. Are there more or less than 5 gal of blood in a human adult?

_____   _____

# Customary Units of Capacity

Choose the most appropriate unit or units to measure the capacity of each. Write tsp, tbsp, fl oz, c, pt, qt, or gal.

1. teacup _____   2. juice box _____

3. motor oil _____   4. salt in a recipe _____

5. carton of cream _____   6. large watering can _____

7. **Number Sense** Would a teaspoon be a good way to measure the capacity of a milk carton? Explain.

_____

_____

_____

8. A jug for the baseball team holds 20 gal of water. To make an energy drink, 1 c of mix is used for every 2 gal of water. How many cups of the mix are needed to fill the jug with energy drink? _____

9. Which unit has the greatest capacity?

   **A** Tablespoon   **C** Pint

   **B** Quart   **D** Teaspoon

10. **Writing to Explain** Cassidy says that capacity is the same as the amount. Do you agree? Explain why or why not.

_____

_____

_____

_____

Name _____

# Units of Weight

There are 16 ounces (oz) in 1 pound (lb).

There are 2,000 lb in 1 ton (T).

| You use ounces to weigh smaller things, like a tomato. | You use pounds to weigh things like a heavy box. | You use tons to weigh very large or heavy things, like a rocket. |

tomato

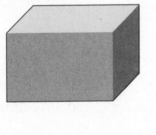

---

Choose the most appropriate unit to measure the weight of each.
Write oz, lb, or T.

**1.** car _____    **2.** computer _____

**3.** bowling ball _____    **4.** onion _____

**5.** Tyrannosaurus rex _____    **6.** vacuum cleaner _____

**7. Reasoning** A hippo weighs about 5,000 lb. Does the same hippo weigh more or less than 5,000 oz?

_____

**8.** Would you most likely measure a leaf using ounces, pounds, or tons? Explain.

_____

_____

_____

Name _____

# Units of Weight

Choose the most appropriate unit to measure the weight of each.
Write oz, lb, or T.

1. truck _____   2. can of vegetables _____

3. person _____   4. desk _____

5. trailer full of bricks _____   6. cup of flour _____

7. box of paper _____   8. CD _____

9. **Reasoning** Would a scale that is used to weigh food be the best tool to weigh concrete blocks? Explain why or why not.

_____

_____

_____

10. Jen wants to weigh her cat. What is the most appropriate unit she should use to weigh the cat, ounces, pounds, or tons? _____

11. What is the most appropriate unit you would use to measure the weight of a house? _____

12. Which animal would it be appropriate to measure its weight in ounces?

    **A** mouse         **B** elephant         **C** horse         **D** cow

13. **Writing to Explain** Dezi says that there are more ounces in 1 T than there are pounds. Do you agree? Explain.

_____

_____

_____

# Changing Customary Units

Here is a table of the customary units of length, capacity, and weight. Use the table to change one customary unit of measure to another.

| Customary Units | | |
|---|---|---|
| **Length** | **Capacity** | **Weight** |
| 1 ft = 12 in. | 1 tbsp = 3 tsp | 1 lb = 16 oz |
| 1 yd = 36 in. | 1 fl oz = 2 tbsp | 1 T = 2,000 lb |
| 1 yd = 3 ft | 1 c = 8 fl oz | |
| 1 mi = 5,280 ft | 1 pt = 2 c | |
| 1 mi = 1,760 yd | 1 qt = 2 pt | |
| | 1 gal = 4 qt | |

Remember: When converting from lesser to greater units, you divide. When converting from greater to lesser units, you multiply.

Which distance is longer, 100 in. or 10 yd?

1 yd = 3 ft    3 ft (12 in./ft) = 36 in.
10 yd at (36 in./yd ) = 360 in.

360 in. is larger than 100 in., so 10 yd is longer.

1. Which is longer, 6 ft or 70 in.? _____

2. How many pints is 24 quarts? _____

3. Which weighs more, 5 lb or 100 oz? _____

4. If a recipe calls for 2 tbsp, how many tsp is that? _____

Name _____

# Changing Customary Units

For **1** through **12**, compare. Write >, <, or = for each ◯.

**1.** 1 yd ◯ 4 ft

**2.** 40 in. ◯ 1 yd

**3.** 6 pt ◯ 3 qt

**4.** 3 lb ◯ 50 oz

**5.** 2 yd ◯ 6 ft

**6.** 3 ft ◯ 30 in.

**7.** 1 gal ◯ 15 c

**8.** 3 T ◯ 3,000 lb

**9.** 1 mi ◯ 2,000 yd

**10.** 100 ft ◯ 100 mi

**11.** 1 gal ◯ 100 fl oz

**12.** 3 tbsp ◯ 10 tsp

**13.** Which measurement is **NOT** equal to 1 mile?

**A** 1,760 yd     **B** 5,280 yd     **C** 5,280 ft     **D** 63,360 in.

**14. Writing to Explain** A recipe calls for 4 tsp of baking soda and 1 fl oz of vanilla. Which measurement is greater? Explain.

_____

_____

_____

# Problem Solving:
# Writing to Explain

Explaining your problem-solving strategy can help you solve
problems and avoid errors.

Jessy and Dean each measured the weight of their pets. Jessy's dog
weighs 12 pounds 2 ounces. Dean's cat weighs 128 ounces. Dean said
his cat weighed more. Is he correct?

| **PLAN** | First, I need to convert Jessy's measurement to ounces so I can compare the weights of her dog and Dean's cat. | Jessy's measurement:  12 pounds 2 ounces<br>I remember that 1 pound = 16 ounces.<br>12 pounds x 16 ounces = 192 ounces.<br>So, 12 pounds 2 ounces = 192 ounces + 2 ounces<br>192 + 2 = 194 ounces |
|---|---|---|
| **SOLVE** | Compare measurements. Dean's cat weighs 128 ounces. Jessy's dog weighs 194 ounces. | Dean was incorrect. His cat weighs 128 ounces and Jessy's dog weighs 194 ounces. Jessy's dog weighs more. Dean may not have remembered that each pound equals 16 ounces. |

Solve the problems below and explain how you found your answers.

1. Raul measures the length of a hallway upstairs as 8 feet. His
   brother measures the length of a hallway downstairs as
   96 inches. Which hallway is longer?

   _____

   _____

   _____

   _____

2. **Number Sense** Sue knows that the perimeter of the
   triangle to the right is 13 inches. Can she find the length
   of the missing side? Explain.

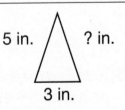

5 in.    ? in.

3 in.

   _____

   _____

   _____

Name _____

# Problem Solving: Writing to Explain

1. The shape to the right is a rectangle. How can you use the information shown to find its perimeter?

   Area = 35 in.²

   |←——— 7 in. ———→|

   _____

   _____

2. David took a survey of 12 people to find out what their favorite animal is. Of those, $\frac{1}{3}$ of the people said they like dogs best. How can you find out how many people liked dogs best?

   _____

   _____

3. Between 6 A.M. and 10 A.M. the temperature rose by 5°F. Between 10 A.M. and 2 P.M. the temperature rose by 6°F. Between 2 P.M. and 6 P.M. the temperature rose by 0°C. Would you be able to tell how much the temperature rose since 6 A.M.? Why or why not?

   _____

   _____

4. How could you find out which weighs more, one ton of pillows or one ton of bowling balls?

   _____

   _____

5. Warren measured a rectangular window to find out how much plastic he would need to cover it. The window measured 5 ft 6 inches by 2 ft 9 inches. About how many square inches of plastic does Warren need to cover the window?

   **A** 1,800 square inches          **C** 2,400 square inches

   **B** 2,100 square inches          **D** 2,800 square inches

Name _____

# Using Metric Units of Length

Metric units are used to estimate and measure length.

**Metric Units of Length**

1 cm = 10 mm

1 dm = 10 cm

1 m = 100 cm

1 km = 1,000 m

Find the length to the nearest centimeter.

Measured to the nearest centimeter, the segment is 6 cm long.

Choose the most appropriate unit to measure each. Write mm, cm, dm, m, or km.

**1.** length of a finger _____

**2.** length of a football _____

**3.** width of a big toe _____

**4.** length of the lunchroom _____

**5.** distance between Paris and London _____

Estimate first. Then, find each length to the nearest centimeter.

**6.** ├────────────────┤   _____ , _____

**7.** ├────────┤   _____ , _____

**8. Number Sense** The distance across a field is 20 m. Is the distance across the same field greater than or less than 20 km?

_____

Name _____

# Using Metric Units of Length

Choose the most appropriate unit to measure each. Write mm, cm, dm, m, or km.

1. width of a house

_____

2. distance across Lake Erie

_____

3. width of a thumbtack

_____

4. thickness of a phone book

_____

Estimate first. Then, find each length to the nearest centimeter.

5. |———————————|

_____ , _____

6. |——————|

_____ , _____

7. **Number Sense** Which would you be more likely to measure in centimeters, a fish tank or a swimming pool?

_____

8. Which is longer, a 12 cm pencil or a 1 dm pen? _____

9. Which is the most appropriate measure for the length of a skateboard?

**A** 5 mm          **B** 5 cm          **C** 5 dm          **D** 5 m

10. **Writing to Explain** Jill measured the length of her eraser. She wrote 5 on her paper without the unit. Which metric unit of measure should Jill include?

_____

_____

_____

Name _____

# Metric Units of Capacity

Capacity is the amount of liquid that an object can hold. The metric system of measurement uses the units liter (L) and milliliter (mL).

You would use liters to measure the amount of water in a water bottle or the amount of gasoline in a gas can.

A milliliter is a very small unit of measurement. There are 5 mL of liquid in a teaspoon. You would use milliliters to measure small amounts of liquid, such as measuring how much medicine to give a baby.

1 L is the same as 1,000 mL.

Choose the most appropriate unit to use to measure the capacity of each. Write L or mL.

1. thimble _____

2. kitchen sink _____

3. coffee cup _____

4. bucket of water for a horse _____

5. **Number Sense** A container holds 5 L of fluid. Does it hold more than or less than 5 mL of fluid?

_____

6. A bottle is filled with saline solution for eyes. Is the bottle more likely to hold 15 mL of solution or 1 L of solution?

_____

Name _____

# Metric Units of Capacity

Choose the most appropriate unit to measure the capacity
of each. Write L or mL.

1. water in a bathtub

2. perfume in a bottle

3. soup in a can

_____ _____ _____

4. **Number Sense** Which will be less, the number of
liters or the number of milliliters, of water in a pool? _____

5. Name something you might measure in liters.

_____

6. Name something you might measure in milliliters.

_____

7. A gallon of milk is about the same as 4 L of milk.
About how many liters of milk are there in 10 gal? _____

8. A small can of tomato juice contains 56 mL
of juice. A large can of tomato juice contains
202 mL of juice. How much juice is there in the
large and small can combined? _____

9. Which capacity would you be most likely to measure in milliliters?

   A  gas in a car

   C  tea in a cup

   B  water in a bathtub

   D  detergent in a bottle

10. **Writing to Explain** Would you be more likely to measure the
amount of water in your kitchen sink in liters or milliliters? Explain.

_____

_____

# Units of Mass

The metric units for mass are grams (g) and kilograms (kg).

$1 \text{ kg} = 1{,}000 \text{ g}$

A cherry or a pen might have a mass of 1 g.

A kitten or watermelon might have a mass of 1 kg.

Choose the most appropriate unit to measure the mass of each.
Write g or kg.

**1.** lawn mower _____

**2.** pumpkin _____

**3.** child _____

**4.** gold ring _____

**5.** robin's egg _____

**6.** cannonball _____

**7.** cement block _____

**8.** spool of thread _____

**9. Number Sense** Which is greater, 850 g or 1 kg?

_____

**10.** The mass of a certain window is 18 kg. What is the mass of
5 of those windows?

_____

_____

**11.** The mass of a horse is 180 kg. The mass of a second
horse is 275 kg. How much larger is the mass of the
second horse than that of the first horse?

_____

_____

_____

# Units of Mass

Choose the most appropriate unit to measure the mass of each.
Write g or kg.

1. banana _____

2. tractor _____

3. coin _____

4. bowling ball _____

5. letter _____

6. encyclopedia _____

7. **Number Sense** Which is a greater number, the mass of a
cat in grams or the mass of the same cat in kilograms?

_____

8. The *Dromornis stirtoni* was once the largest
living bird. It is now extinct. The ostrich is
now the largest living bird. What is the
difference in mass between the *Dromornis
stirtoni* and the ostrich?

_____

| Bird | Mass |
|------|------|
| Ostrich | 156 kg |
| Andean condor | 9 kg |
| Eurasian eagle owl | 4.2 kg |
| *Dromornis stirtoni* | 454 kg |

9. Which has a larger mass, an Andean condor or a Eurasian
eagle owl?

_____

10. Which object would be most likely to have a mass of 2 kg?

**A** A truck          **B** An orange          **C** A mosquito          **D** A math book

11. **Writing to Explain** Would you be more likely to find the
mass of a pen in grams or in kilograms? Explain.

_____

_____

_____

Name ______________________________



# Changing Metric Units

Here is a table of the conversion factors for metric units.

Metric Measures

1 cm = 10 mm
1 dm = 10 cm
1 m = 100 cm
1 m = 1,000 mm
1 km = 1,000 m
1 L = 1,000 mL
1 kg = 1,000 g

Remember: When converting from lesser to greater units you divide. When converting from greater to lesser units you multiply.

Which has more mass, a kilogram of lead or 1,200 grams of bricks?

1 kg = 1,000 g
1,000 g of lead is less than 1,200 g of bricks.
**The bricks have more mass.**

Solve.

**1.** Which is greater, 200 mm or 1 m? ______________

**2.** Which amount is less 250 mL or 250 L? ______________

**3.** If 4 apples have a mass of 1 kg, about how many grams is each apple? ______________

# Changing Metric Units

For **1** through **12**, compare. Write >, <, or = for each ◯.

1.  4 m ◯ 400 dm       2.  4 dm ◯ 40 cm

3.  10 L ◯ 1,000 mL   4.  2 kg ◯ 1,500 g

5.  15 cm ◯ 150 mm   6.  1 km ◯ 999 m

7.  4 L ◯ 4,500 mL     8.  500 g ◯ 5 kg

9.  6 km ◯ 6,000 m   10.  200 cm ◯ 3 m

11.  3,000 m ◯ 2 km   12.  100 mm ◯ 1 dm

13. Which measurement is **NOT** equal to 3 m?

 **A** 30 dm       **B** 300 cm       **C** 3,000 mm       **D** 3,000 cm

14. **Writing to Explain** If 5 potatoes together have a mass
 of 1 kilogram and 8 pears together have a mass of 1,200
 grams, which has the greater mass, a potato or a pear?
 Explain.

 _____

 _____

 _____

# Units of Time

You can use the information in the table to compare different amounts of time. For example:

Which is longer, 3 years or 40 months?

According to the table, 1 year = 12 months.

1 year = 12 months
3 years = 36 months

$$\begin{array}{r} 12 \\ \times\ 3 \\ \hline 36 \end{array}$$

40 months > 36 months
40 months > 3 years

So, 40 months is longer than 3 years.

| Units of Time |
|---|
| 1 minute = 60 seconds |
| 1 hour = 60 minutes |
| 1 day = 24 hours |
| 1 week = 7 days |
| 1 month = about 4 weeks |
| 1 year = 52 weeks |
| 1 year = 12 months |
| 1 year = 365 days |
| 1 leap year = 366 days |
| 1 decade = 10 years |
| 1 century = 100 years |
| 1 millennium = 1,000 years |

Write <, >, or = for each ◯.

**1.** 1 year ◯ 350 days

**2.** 25 months ◯ 2 years

**3.** 20 decades ◯ 2 centuries

**4.** 720 days ◯ 2 years

**5.** 8 decades ◯ 1 century

**6.** 72 hours ◯ 3 days

**7.** 240 minutes ◯ 3 hours

**8.** 3 years ◯ 120 months

**9. Number Sense** How many hours are in 2 days? _____

**10.** A score is 20 years. How many years is 5 score? _____

**11.** Dave's goldfish lived for 2 years, 8 months. Chris's goldfish lived for 35 months. Whose goldfish lived longer? _____

**12.** Tree A lived for 6 decades and 5 years. Tree B lived for 58 years. Which tree lived longer? _____

Name _____

# Units of Time

Write >, <, or = for each ◯.

1. 48 hours ◯ 4 days

2. 1 year ◯ 12 months

3. 60 minutes ◯ 2 hours

4. 17 days ◯ 2 weeks

5. 5 months ◯ 40 weeks

6. 1 millennium ◯ 10 centuries

7. 6 decades ◯ 1 century

8. 5 decades ◯ 48 years

9. Cheryl's grandparents have been married for 6 decades. How many years have they been married?

_____

10. Tom was in elementary school from 1997 to 2002. How much time was that in years?

_____

The Declaration of Independence was signed on July 4, 1776. The United States celebrated the bicentennial on July 4, 1976. How much time was that in

11. years? _____

12. decades? _____

13. 49 days = ☐

   **A** 5 weeks      **B** 6 weeks      **C** 7 weeks      **D** 8 weeks

14. **Writing to Explain** Which is longer: 180 sec or 3 min? Explain how you decided.

_____

_____

_____

# Problem Solving:
# Work Backward

**Morning Routine** Brenda takes 30 minutes to get dressed for school. She eats breakfast for 20 minutes more, then walks to school. It takes Brenda 15 minutes to walk to school. Brenda needs to be at school by 8:55 A.M. What time is the latest she should get out of bed in the morning?

### Read and Understand

**Step 1: What do you know?**

Brenda takes 30 min to get ready, 20 min for breakfast, and 15 min to walk to school. She must be at school by 8:55 A.M.

**Step 2: What are you trying to find?**

What time is the latest Brenda should get up?

### Plan and Solve

**Step 3: What strategy will you use?**

**Strategy:** Work backward.

**Work backward from the end, doing the opposite of each step.**

I need to work backward, or subtract from the school arrival time, one step at a time.

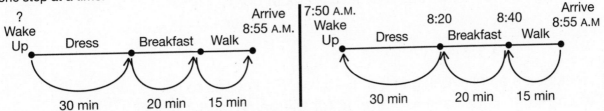

Brenda must get up by 7:50 A.M. at the latest to make it to school on time.

### Look Back and Check

**Step 4: Is your work correct?**

Yes. If I follow the times forward, I end at 8:55 A.M.

1. When Christopher Columbus was 41 years old he sailed across the Atlantic Ocean for the first time. He went on his final expedition 10 years later, which took 2 years. He died 2 years after his final expedition ended, in 1506. What year was Columbus born?

Name _____

# Problem Solving: Work Backward

Solve by working backward. Write the answer in a complete sentence.

1. There were 21 students in Travis's fourth-grade class at the end of the school year. During the year four new students joined his class, and 2 moved away. One student was transferred to another fourth-grade teacher. How many students were in Travis's class at the beginning of the school year?

   _____

   _____

   _____

2. Sir John Franklin was an explorer who traveled in Canada and the United States. He was 33 years old when he began exploring northwestern Canada. In a second expedition 17 years later, he explored as far as Alaska. 11 years later, Franklin died in an expedition in search of a Northwest Passage in 1847. In what year was Franklin born?

   _____

3. Tessie has a volleyball game at 6:45 P.M. She needs to be there 15 minutes early to warm up for the game, and it takes her 40 minutes to get to the gym. What time should she leave her house?

   _____

4. Frank bought lunch for $5.60 at a diner. He spent $2.00 to ride the bus to the mall and back, and spent $6.50 while he was at the mall. His friend Bill paid him back $5.00 that he had borrowed last week. If Frank arrived at home with $10.50 in his pocket, how much did he have when he left home that morning?

   _____

Name _____

# Solving Perimeter and Area Problems

1. Find the length of the rectangle.

   $A =$ _____ and $w =$ _____

   $A = \ell \times w$

   _____ $= \ell \times$ _____

   (Think: If $63 = \ell \times 7$, then $\ell =$ _____ ÷ _____ )

   $\ell =$ _____

   So the length is _____ feet.

   7 ft | Area = 63 sq ft

   $\ell$

2. Find the width of the rectangle.

   $P =$ _____ and $\ell =$ _____

   $P = 2\ell + 2w$

   _____ $= (2 \times$ _____ $) + 2w$

   _____ $=$ _____ $+ 2w$ (Think: If $30 = 22 + 2w$, then $2w =$ _____ − _____

   $2w =$ _____ (Think: If $2 \times w = 8$, then $w =$ _____ ÷ _____

   $w =$ _____

   So the width is _____ inches.

   $w$ | Perimeter = 30 in.

   11 in.

# Solving Perimeter and Area Problems

Use the formulas for perimeter and area of rectangles to solve each problem.

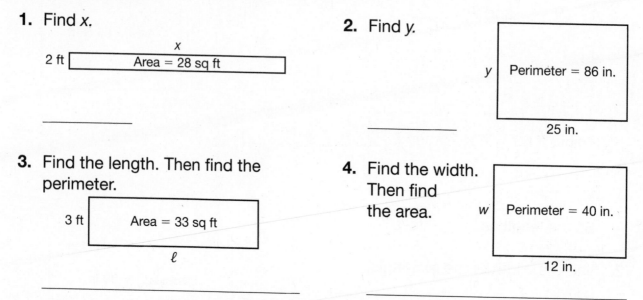

**1.** Find *x*.

2 ft | Area = 28 sq ft | (x on top)

_____

**2.** Find *y*.

y | Perimeter = 86 in.

25 in.

_____

**3.** Find the length. Then find the perimeter.

3 ft | Area = 33 sq ft
ℓ

_____

**4.** Find the width. Then find the area.

w | Perimeter = 40 in.

12 in.

_____

Michael designs and makes quilts. Answer questions **5–8** about the dimensions of his quilts. You may wish to use a sketch to help you solve the problem.

**5.** He made a baby quilt that was 3 feet wide. Its perimeter was 16 feet. What was its area?

_____

**6.** He made a queen-sized quilt that was 8 feet long. Its area was 64 square feet. What was its perimeter?

_____

**7. Reason** He wanted to make another quilt with an area of 42 square feet. What are its possible dimensions if they must be whole numbers? Which length and width makes the most sense for a quilt?

_____

_____

**8. Persevere** The perimeter of another quilt had to be 34 feet because he only had that much binding. If he wanted it to be 8 feet long, what would its area be?

**A** 18 sq ft          **B** 72 sq ft          **C** 144 sq ft          **D** 292 sq ft

# Solving Measurement Problems

Lance has a 5-gallon aquarium. He fills the aquarium using a
2-quart container. How many times will he have to fill the 2-quart
container to fill the aquarium?

Use a bar diagram to see how the units are related.

| 1 gal | | | |
|---|---|---|---|
| 1 qt | 1 qt | | |

4 qt = 1 gal or 2 qt = $\frac{1}{2}$ gal.

So, Lance has to fill the container 2 times to fill one gallon in the
aquarium.

Since there are 5 gallons, he must fill the container 2 × 5, or
10 times.

In **1–2**, use the diagram shown to help solve the problem.

1. It took Amber 5 hours 16 minutes to finish a race. Her time at
   the halfway marker was 2 hours 49 minutes. How long did it
   take Amber to complete the second half of the race?

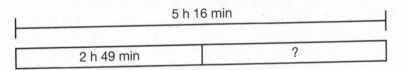

   1 h = _____ min, so 5 h 16 min = 4 h _____ min

   4 h 76 min − 2 h 49 min = _____

2. **Reason** Jeremy uses 18 inches of twine for each box he packs for shipping.
   How many yards of twine does he need to wrap 5 boxes?

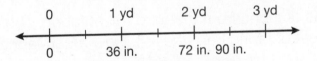

Name _____

# Solving Measurement Problems

In **1**, use the diagram shown to help solve the problem.

**1.** Tawny has $2\frac{1}{2}$ pints of juice. She has juice glasses that hold 5 fluid ounces. How many glasses can she fill with juice?

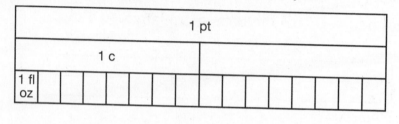

_____

In **2–5**, draw a diagram to help solve each problem.

**2. Reason** A race is 10 kilometers long. Markers will be placed at the beginning and end of the race-course and at each 500-meter mark. How many markers are needed to mark the course for the race?

_____

**3.** On Monday, students at a summer camp spent 4 hours 25 minutes at the pool learning to swim. In the morning they spent 2 hours 48 minutes at the pool. How long did the students spend at the pool in the afternoon?

_____

**4. Persevere** The mass of a tiger at a zoo is 135 kilograms. Randy's cat has a mass of 5,000 grams. How many times greater is the mass of the tiger than the mass of Randy's cat?

_____

**5.** Lou cuts $2\frac{1}{3}$ yards of fabric from a 9-yard roll of fabric. Then he cuts 4 more feet of fabric from the roll. How much fabric is left on the roll?

**A** $3\frac{2}{3}$ yd      **B** $5\frac{1}{3}$ yd      **C** $6\frac{1}{3}$ yd      **D** $6\frac{2}{3}$ yd

Name _____

# Solving Problems Involving Money

Christine buys a loaf of bread from the bakery that costs $3.59. She pays for the loaf with a $5 bill. What is Christine's change?

First, start with the cost of the bread. Use coins and bills until you reach the amount Christine paid.

$3.59 →     $3.60 →     $3.65 →     $3.75 →     $4.00 →     $5.00

Second, count the change. Count coins and bills in reverse order.
$1.00 → $1.25 → $1.35 → $1.40 → $1.41

Christine's change is $1.41.

---

List the coins and bills you would use to make the amount of change for each situation. Then tell the amount of change.

1. Bryce bought a map that cost $7.35. He used a $10 bill to pay for the map. What is his change?

   _____

2. Nora bought a pair of running shoes that cost $34.29. She paid for the shoes with two $20 bills. What is her change?

   _____

3. **Reason** Orlando bought some groceries that cost a total of $22.68. He used a $20 bill and a $10 bill to pay for the groceries. What are two different ways he could receive his change? What is his change?

   _____

   _____

Name _____

# Solving Problems Involving Money

Tell the amount of change for each situation.

1. Kyle bought a DVD that cost $19.23, including tax. She gave the sales clerk a $20 bill. How much change should Kyle receive?

   _____

2. **Mental Math** Sean uses a $5 bill and two quarters to pay for a souvenir mug that costs $4.35. What is his change?

   _____

3. Zooey bought a new skateboard that costs $36.79. How much change should she get if she paid for the skateboard with two $20-bills?

   _____

4. **Reason** Vince buys a model train that costs $6.55. Why might he give the salesperson a $10 bill and a nickel? What is his change?

   _____

5. **Critique Reasoning** Julia spent $7.36 on lunch. She gave the cashier two $5 bills to pay the bill and received $2.54 in change. Did she receive the correct change? Explain.

   _____

6. **Reason** Brad paid for a book that cost $13.40 with a $20 bill. What is the least combination of coins and bills that can be used to make his change? What are two other different combinations of coins and bills that can be used to make the change?

   _____

   _____

7. Emma buys a game for $26.84. She pays for the game with a $20 bill and two $5 bills. How much change should she receive?

   **A** $1.84         **B** $3.16         **C** $3.26         **D** $3.84

# Solving Problems Involving Line Plots

Eight people in a class measured the length of their steps and got the following measurements: 1.6 feet, 1.8 feet, 1.9 feet, 1.7 feet, 1.9 feet, 1.8 feet, 1.8 feet, and 1.7 feet.

Draw a number line. Start with the least measurement and end with the greatest measurement.

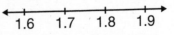

What is the most common step length?

What is the difference between the greatest step length and the least step length?

Add your data to the line plot. Use Xs to show each measurement. Give the line plot a title.

**Length of Steps in Feet**

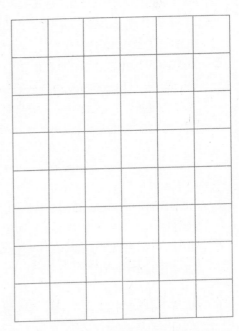

You can draw a line plot to find out.

The most common step length is 1.8 feet. The difference between the greatest step length and least step length is 0.3 feet.

---

For **1–3**, use the data set below which lists the number of books each student in Mr. Kent's class read in the last month.

$2, 2\frac{1}{2}, 3\frac{1}{2}, 3, 4, 3\frac{1}{2}, 2, 3\frac{1}{2}, 4, 3\frac{1}{2}, 4\frac{1}{2}, 3\frac{1}{2}$

1. Make a line plot of the data.

2. What is the most common number of books read in the last month?

_____

3. **Use tools** What is the difference between the greatest and least number of books read?

_____

# Solving Problems Involving Line Plots

For **1–4,** use the data set below which lists the length of time in seconds it takes for each student in Ms. Sousa's class to say the alphabet.

$5, 4, 4\frac{1}{2}, 6, 5, 6\frac{1}{2}, 5\frac{1}{2}, 7, 5\frac{1}{2}, 7\frac{1}{2}, 6, 4\frac{1}{2}, 4\frac{1}{2}, 4\frac{1}{2}, 4, 6, 4\frac{1}{2}, 5\frac{1}{2}, 5, 6\frac{1}{2}$

1. Make a line plot of the data.

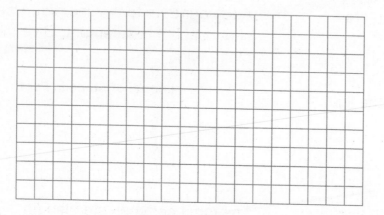

2. **Use Tools** What is the most common time it takes a student to say the alphabet?

_____

3. **Writing to Explain** Yuri says that the difference between the least amount of time it takes a student to say the alphabet and the greatest amount of time is $4\frac{1}{2}$ seconds. Do you agree? Explain.

_____

_____

_____

4. **Reason** A new student joins Ms. Sousa's class. That student can say the alphabet in $3\frac{1}{2}$ seconds. What is the new difference between the greatest length of time and the least length of time?

   **A** $4\frac{1}{2}$ seconds   **B** 4 seconds   **C** $3\frac{1}{2}$ seconds   **D** 3 seconds

# Problem Solving: Solve a Simpler Problem and Make a Table

**Squares** A student is making a pattern of squares out of cotton balls. Each unit on a side of the pattern is made up of 2 cotton balls. How many cotton balls will the student need to make a pattern that is 4 units high and 4 units wide?

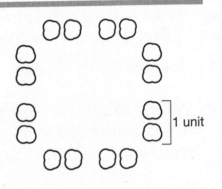

1 unit

### Read and Understand

**Step 1:** What do you know?
There are 2 cotton balls in each unit. The square is 4 units high and 4 units wide.

**Step 2:** What are you trying to find?
How many cotton balls are needed in all.

### Plan and Solve

**Step 3:** What strategy will you use?

**Problem 1:** How many cotton balls are needed for a 1-unit by 1-unit square?

8 cotton balls are needed for a 1-unit square.

**Strategy: Solve a simpler problem.**

**Problem 2:** How many cotton balls are needed for a 2-unit by 2-unit square?

16 cotton balls are needed for a 2-unit square.

There are 2 cotton balls for each unit on the side.
There are always 4 sides, so the pattern is the
number of units in each side, multiplied by 2 cotton balls, multiplied by 4 sides.

| Square units | $1 \times 1$ | $2 \times 2$ | $4 \times 4$ |
| --- | --- | --- | --- |
| Cotton balls needed | 8 | 16 | 32 |

**Answer: 32 cotton balls are needed.**

### Look Back and Check

**Step 4:** Is your work correct?
Yes, all of my computations are correct, and I saw the correct pattern.

1. Joan works for 6 hr each weekday, and 8 hr total on the weekends. She earns $6 an hour on weekdays and $9 an hour on weekends. How much money does she earn each week?

_____

_____

# Problem Solving:
# Solve a Simpler Problem
# and Make a Table

Sam needs to cut a piece of sheet metal into 8 pieces. It takes him 5 minutes to make each cut.

1. How many cuts will Sam make? _____

2. **Writing to Explain** How would making a table help you to find the number of minutes it took Sam to cut the sheet metal into 8 pieces?

_____

_____

3. How long will it take Sam to turn the sheet metal into 8 pieces? Write your answer in a complete sentence.

_____

Sarah is having a slumber party with her 11 friends and they are telling scary stories. They divide into 3 groups and each group tells a story. Each group member talks for 3 minutes.

4. How many people are in each group? _____

5. How many minutes does each group take to tell a story? _____

6. How many minutes does it take for all three groups to tell their stories? _____

7. If Sarah divided her friends into 4 groups and each person still got the same time to talk, how long would it take to tell the stories?

    **A** 16 minutes    **B** 36 minutes    **C** 48 minutes    **D** 144 minutes

# Points, Lines, and Planes

Here are some important geometric terms.

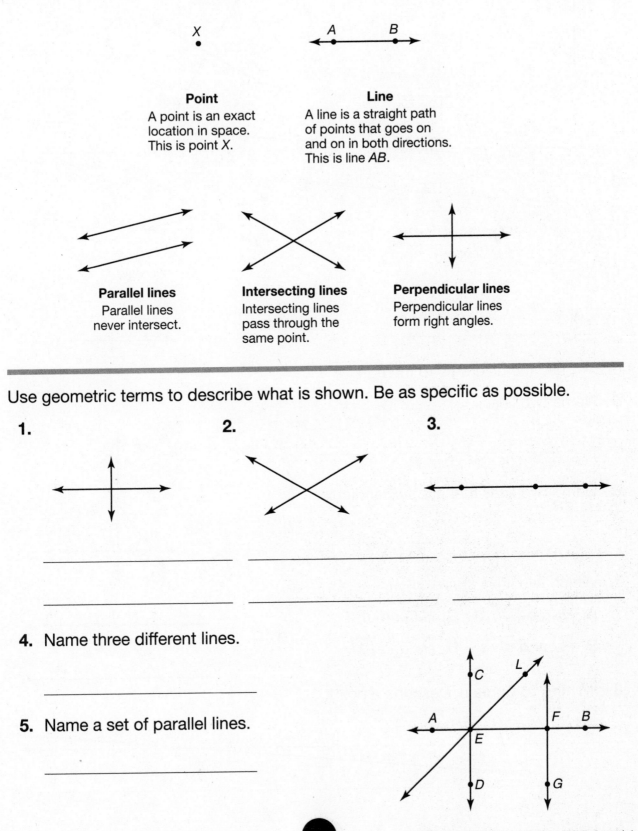

**Point**
A point is an exact location in space. This is point $X$.

**Line**
A line is a straight path of points that goes on and on in both directions. This is line $AB$.

**Parallel lines**
Parallel lines never intersect.

**Intersecting lines**
Intersecting lines pass through the same point.

**Perpendicular lines**
Perpendicular lines form right angles.

Use geometric terms to describe what is shown. Be as specific as possible.

1.

_____

_____

2.

_____

_____

3.

_____

_____

4. Name three different lines.

_____

5. Name a set of parallel lines.

_____

Name _____

# Points, Lines, and Planes

Use geometric terms to describe what is shown. Be as specific as possible.

1.

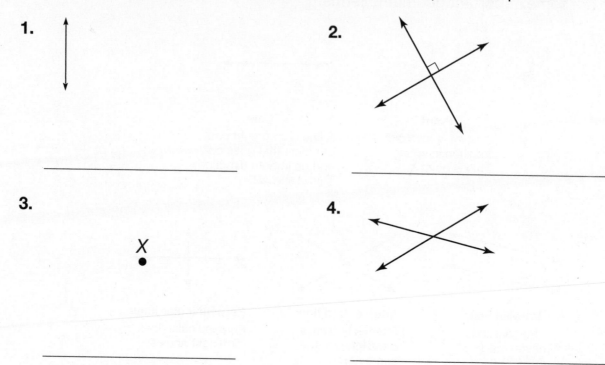

2.

_____

3.

X
●

4.

_____

For **5–7,** use the diagrams to the right.

5. Name two lines.

_____

6. Name two lines that are perpendicular.

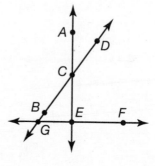

_____

7. Which two lines are parallel?

  **A** $\overleftrightarrow{HK}$ and $\overleftrightarrow{JL}$    **C** $\overleftrightarrow{HJ}$ and $\overrightarrow{JK}$

  **B** $\overleftrightarrow{HJ}$ and $\overrightarrow{JL}$    **D** $\overleftrightarrow{HJ}$ and $\overleftrightarrow{LM}$

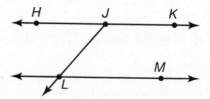

8. **Writing to Explain** Describe a point.

_____

_____

# Line Segments, Rays, and Angles

Here are some important geometric terms.

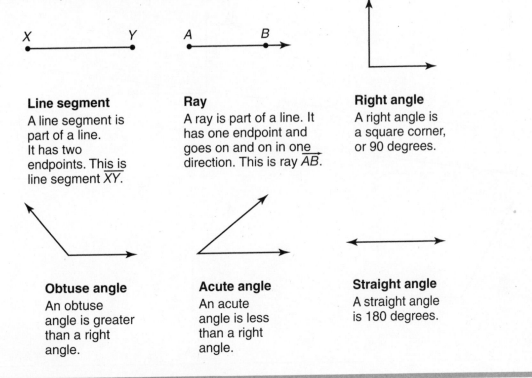

**Line segment**
A line segment is part of a line. It has two endpoints. This is line segment $\overline{XY}$.

**Ray**
A ray is part of a line. It has one endpoint and goes on and on in one direction. This is ray $\overrightarrow{AB}$.

**Right angle**
A right angle is a square corner, or 90 degrees.

**Obtuse angle**
An obtuse angle is greater than a right angle.

**Acute angle**
An acute angle is less than a right angle.

**Straight angle**
A straight angle is 180 degrees.

Use geometric terms to describe what is shown. Be as specific as possible.

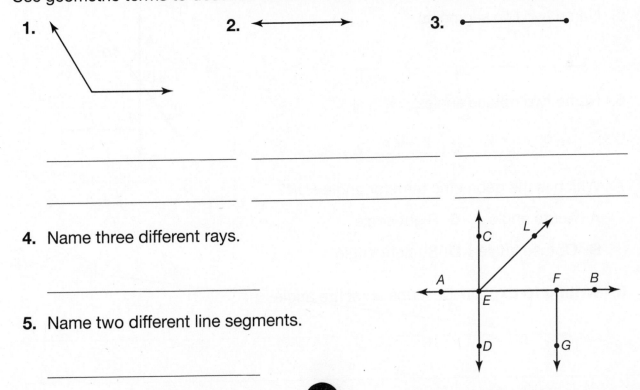

1.

2.

3.

_____

_____

_____

_____

_____

_____

4. Name three different rays.

_____

5. Name two different line segments.

_____

# Line Segments, Rays, and Angles

Use geometric terms to describe what is shown. Be as specific as possible.

1.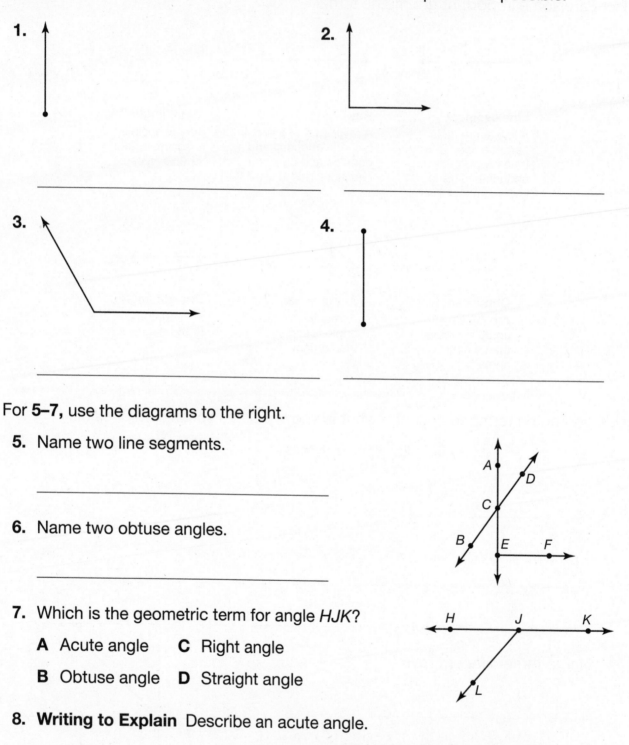

2.

3.

4.

For **5–7,** use the diagrams to the right.

5. Name two line segments.

_____

6. Name two obtuse angles.

_____

7. Which is the geometric term for angle *HJK*?

   **A** Acute angle   **C** Right angle

   **B** Obtuse angle   **D** Straight angle

8. **Writing to Explain** Describe an acute angle.

_____

_____

# Understanding Angles and Unit Angles

You can find the measure of an angle using fractions of a circle.

The angle is $\frac{1}{6}$ of a circle.

What is the measure of this angle?

Divide to find the angle measure of $\frac{1}{6}$ of a circle.

Remember, $\frac{1}{6}$ means 1 of 6 equal parts, so divide by 6 to find the angle measure.

Number of degrees in whole circle ———→ $360° \div 6 = 60°$ ←——— Number of degrees in the angle.

The measure of this angle is ___60___ degrees.

For Exercise **1**, show the work you do to find the measure of the angle.

1. **Use Structure** A circle is divided into 9 equal parts.

   What is the measure of this angle?

   Write an equation using division to find the measure of the angle.

   _____ ÷ _____ = _____

   The measure of this angle is _____ degrees.

2. Janie cut a round slice of watermelon into 5 equal pieces. What is the angle of each piece? Use equivalent fractions.

   The measure of this angle is _____ degrees.

3. Frank cut a pie into 10 equal slices. There are only 3 slices left. What is the measure of the angle for the 3 slices that are left? _____.

4. Maria cut a pizza into 8 equal slices. She put a slice of pizza on 3 plates. What is the measure of the angle for the slices that are left? _____.

# Understanding Angles and Unit Angles

In **1–3,** find the measure of each angle.

1. The angle is $\frac{1}{12}$ of the circle.

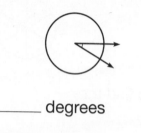

_____ degrees

2. A circle is divided into 20 equal parts. What is the angle measure of three of those parts?

_____ degrees

3. A circle is divided into 9 equal parts. What is the angle measure of two of those parts?

_____ degrees

4. **Reasoning** Kurt cut pizzas into wedges measuring 40 degrees. If each person eats one piece of pizza, how many people could he feed with two whole pizzas?

_____

5. Sam cut a pie into equal slices. There are only 3 slices left. The angle measure for the three slices is 72°. How many slices did Sam cut the pie into?

_____

6. **Writing to Explain** A circle is divided into 18 equal parts. How many degrees is the angle for each part? How many degrees is the angle for 5 parts? Explain.

_____

_____

7. Brian cut an extra large round pizza into 12 pieces. Seven of the pieces were eaten. What angle measure of pizza is left?

**A** 30°        **B** 120°        **C** 150°        **D** 210°

# Measuring with Unit Angles

You can use an angle you know to find the measure of an angle you do not know. Use the smaller angle of the beige pattern block. It has a measure of 30°.

Find the measure of the angle below.

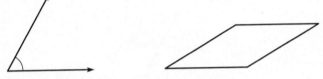

Two of the 30° angles will fit into the angle.

Add: 30° + 30° = 60°. The measure of this angle is 60°.

Use the beige pattern block to find the measure of the angle. Draw lines to show how many 30° angles fit into the angle.

**1.**

_____

**2. Be Precise** Explain how you found the measure of the angle.

_____

_____

_____

_____

# Measuring with Unit Angles

In **1–5,** find the measure of each angle. Use pattern blocks to help.

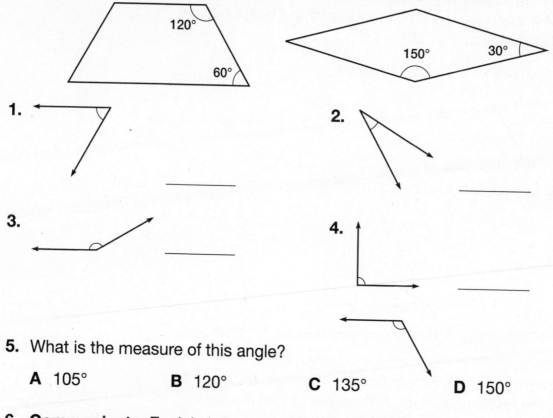

1. _____

2. _____

3. _____

4. _____

5. What is the measure of this angle?

   **A** 105°          **B** 120°          **C** 135°          **D** 150°

6. **Communicate** Explain how you found the measure of the angle in Exercise 3. Use pictures, words, and numbers in your explanation.

   _____

   _____

   _____

   _____

# Measuring Angles

An angle is formed by two rays that meet at a common endpoint called the vertex. The angle is measured in **degrees (°)**.

An angle can be measured or created using a **protractor**.

**To measure an angle:**

Place the protractor's center on the vertex of the angle, and the 0° mark on one of the angle's rays. Read the number in degrees where the other ray of the angle crosses the protractor.

**To create an angle:**

Draw a dot to show the vertex of the angle. Place the center of the protractor on the vertex point. Draw another point at the 0° mark and another point at the angle degree mark. Draw rays from the vertex through the other points.

For Exercises **1** through **3**, measure the angles.

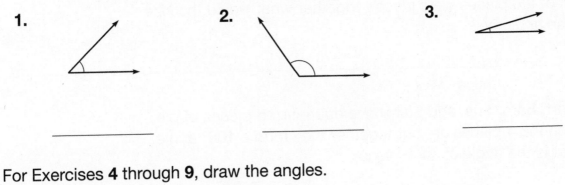

1.

2.

3.

_____        _____        _____

For Exercises **4** through **9**, draw the angles.

**4.** 65°                    **5.** 90°                    **6.** 145°

**7.** 75°                    **8.** 135°                   **9.** 180°

Name _____

# Measuring Angles

For Exercises **1** through **4**, use a protractor to measure the angle.

1. _____  2. _____  3. _____  4. _____

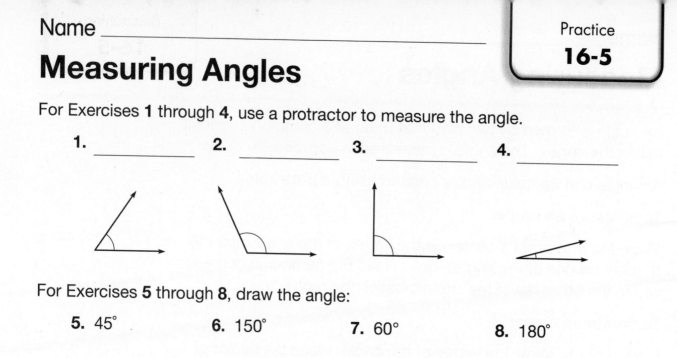

For Exercises **5** through **8**, draw the angle:

**5.** 45°            **6.** 150°            **7.** 60°            **8.** 180°

9. Rich has 3 pieces of pizza. Each pizza end forms a 20° angle.
   If all of the pieces were placed together what would the size
   of the angle be?

   _____

10. Stuart, Sam, Sue, and Sally have equal-sized pieces of pie.
    When the 4 pieces are put together they form a 100° angle.
    What is the angle of each piece?

    **A** 100°          **B** 50°          **C** 25°          **D** 15°

11. **Writing to Explain** Gail and her 3 friends all share half a
    pie. Gail and her friends each eat an equal-sized piece.
    They believe each piece has an angle equal to 25°. Are their
    calculations correct? Explain.

    _____

    _____

    _____

# Adding and Subtracting Angle Measures

You can add to find angle measures.

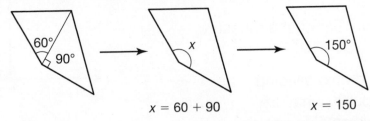

$x = 60 + 90$    $x = 150$

You can subtract to find angle measures.

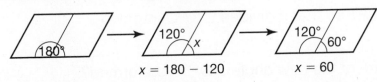

$x = 180 - 120$    $x = 60$

Angles *TUW* and *WUV*, together, make the larger angle, *TUV*. Add or subtract. Write the missing angle measure.

**Angle Measure (°)**

|     | ∠*TUW* | ∠*WUV* | ∠*TUV* |
|-----|--------|--------|--------|
| **1.** | 120 | 45 | |
| **2.** | 105 | | 155 |
| **3.** | 100 | | 170 |
| **4.** | | 25 | 150 |
| **5.** | 112 | 36 | |

6. **Reason** Use the picture at the right. Jody is making a mosaic. She places two pieces along an edge as shown. She needs a third piece to fill the space between these two pieces. What size corner-angle does the third piece need to have in order to fill the space with no gaps?

_____

_____

Name _____

# Adding and Subtracting Angle Measures

Use the diagram. Add or subtract to find the angle measure.

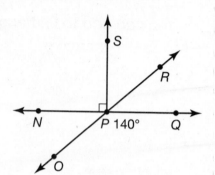

1. What is the measure of ∠NPO? _____

2. What is the measure of ∠SPR if the measure of ∠RPQ is 40°? _____

3. If a line segment PT is drawn dividing ∠SPN into two equal parts, what are the measures of the two smaller angles? _____

4. Use the diagram.

   a. Draw line segment PT so that it divides ∠OPQ into two smaller parts.

   b. What is the measure of the new angle ∠OPT you formed?

   _____

   c. Write an equation and solve it to find the measure of ∠TPQ.

   _____

   _____

5. ∠CMW and ∠WML together form ∠CML. ∠CMW is a right angle. What must be true about ∠CML?

   **A** It is an obtuse angle.

   **B** It is a straight angle.

   **C** Its measure is greater than 90°.

   **D** Its measure is greater than 180°.

6. **Writing to Explain** Use the diagram above. Shane sees that ∠OPN and ∠SPR are both smaller angles within ∠OPR, a straight angle. He says you can subtract the measure of ∠OPN from 180 to find the measure of ∠SPR. Is he right? Explain.

   _____

   _____

   _____

# Polygons

Polygons are closed plane figures that are made up of line segments. All of the line segments connect. All of the sides of a polygon are straight, not curved.

**Polygon**
Closed figure
made of
line segments.

**Not a polygon**
Not a closed
figure.

**Not a polygon**
Not all of the
sides are line
segments.

Here are some common polygons. Note that the sides of polygons do not all have to be the same length.

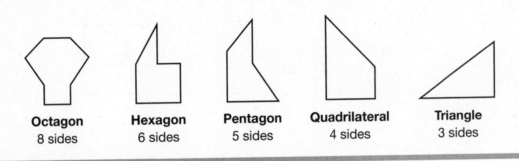

**Octagon**
8 sides

**Hexagon**
6 sides

**Pentagon**
5 sides

**Quadrilateral**
4 sides

**Triangle**
3 sides

Draw an example of each type of polygon.
How many sides and vertices does each
one have?

1. Hexagon

    _____

2. Quadrilateral

    _____

3. Pentagon

    _____

4. Octagon

    _____

# Polygons

Draw an example of each polygon. How many sides and vertices does each one have?

**1.** Quadrilateral      **2.** Octagon      **3.** Hexagon

_____      _____      _____

The map shows the shapes of buildings in Polygon Park. Identify the polygons that are lettered.

**4.** A

_____

**5.** D

_____

**6.** C               **7.** B

_____         _____

**8.** E               **9.** F

_____         _____

**10.** Which is the point where sides meet in a polygon?

     **A** edge      **B** endpoint      **C** side      **D** vertex

**11.** **Writing to Explain** Describe two polygons by the number of vertices and sides each has.

_____

Name _____

# Triangles

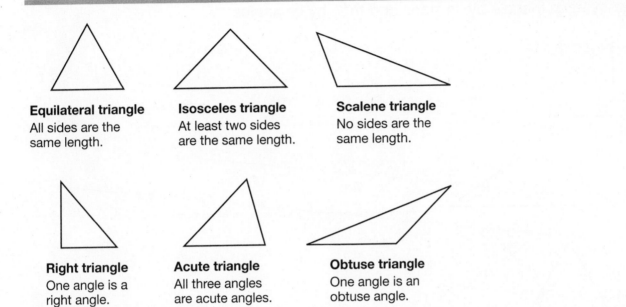

**Equilateral triangle**
All sides are the
same length.

**Isosceles triangle**
At least two sides
are the same length.

**Scalene triangle**
No sides are the
same length.

**Right triangle**
One angle is a
right angle.

**Acute triangle**
All three angles
are acute angles.

**Obtuse triangle**
One angle is an
obtuse angle.

Classify each triangle by its sides and then by its angles.

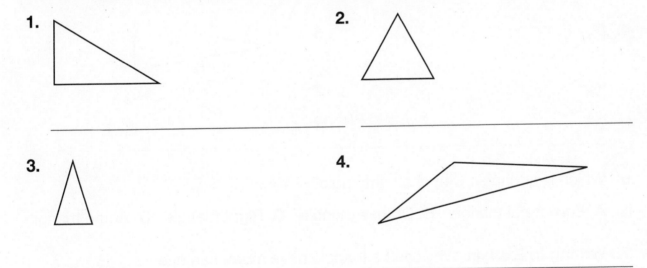

1.

_____

2.

_____

3.

_____

4.

_____

Name _____

# Triangles

Classify each triangle by its sides and then by its angles.

1. 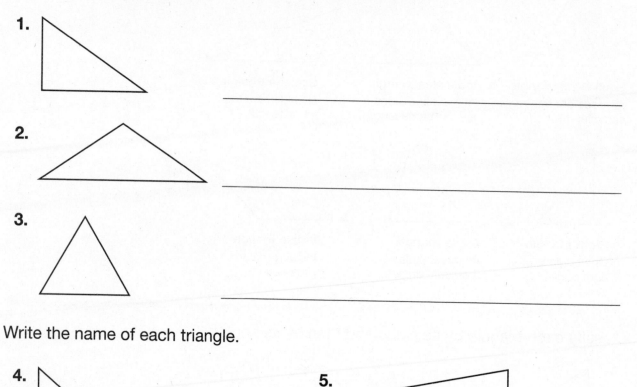 _____

2. _____

3. _____

Write the name of each triangle.

4. _____

5. _____

6. Which is a triangle with one right angle?

  **A** Equilateral triangle  **B** Obtuse triangle  **C** Right triangle  **D** Acute triangle

7. **Writing to Explain** Why can't a triangle have more than one obtuse angle?

_____

_____

_____

# Quadrilaterals

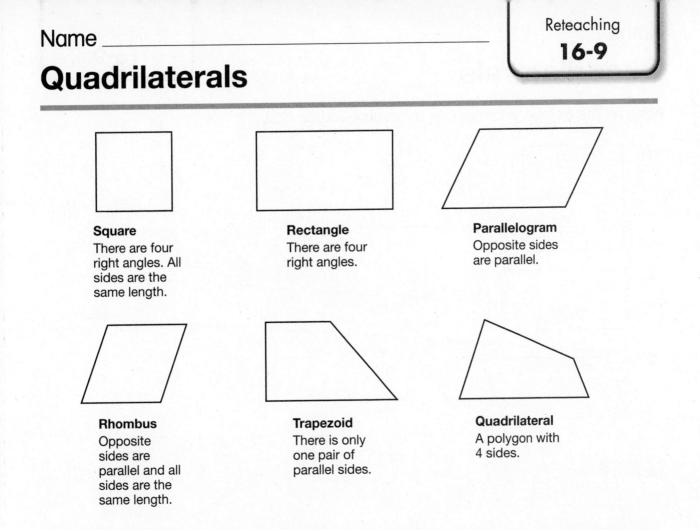

**Square**
There are four right angles. All sides are the same length.

**Rectangle**
There are four right angles.

**Parallelogram**
Opposite sides are parallel.

**Rhombus**
Opposite sides are parallel and all sides are the same length.

**Trapezoid**
There is only one pair of parallel sides.

**Quadrilateral**
A polygon with 4 sides.

---

Write the name of each quadrilateral.

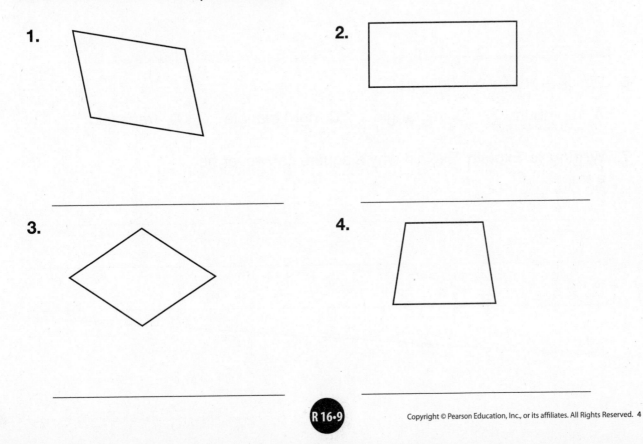

1. _____

2. _____

3. _____

4. _____

# Quadrilaterals

Write all the names you can use for each quadrilateral.

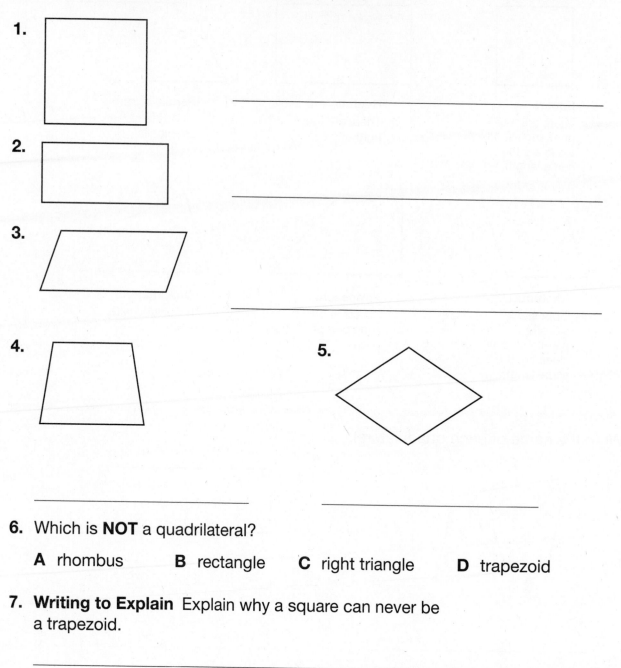

1.

_____

2.

_____

3.

_____

4.

_____

5.

_____

6. Which is **NOT** a quadrilateral?

    **A** rhombus     **B** rectangle     **C** right triangle     **D** trapezoid

7. **Writing to Explain** Explain why a square can never be a trapezoid.

_____

_____

_____

# Line Symmetry

Symmetric figures are figures that can be folded to make two halves that match each other. The lines that divide a symmetric figure into matching parts are called lines of symmetry.

This square has 4 lines of symmetry. If you fold the square along any of the 4 dashed lines, the two halves will lie on top of each other.

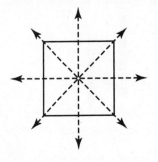

Tell if each line is a line of symmetry.

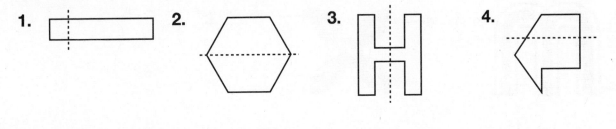

1. _____

2. _____

3. _____

4. _____

Tell how many lines of symmetry each figure has.

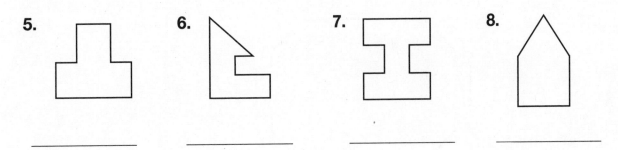

5. _____

6. _____

7. _____

8. _____

9. **Reasoning** How many lines of symmetry does the letter R have?  _____

10. Complete the drawing so that the figure is symmetric.

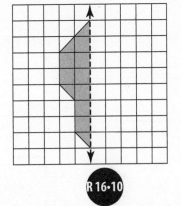

# Line Symmetry

Tell if each line is a line of symmetry.

1. _____

2. _____

3. _____

Tell how many lines of symmetry each figure has.

4. _____

5. _____

6. _____

7. Draw lines of symmetry.

8. How many lines of symmetry does a rhombus that is not a square have?

   **A** 0           **B** 1           **C** 2           **D** 3

9. **Writing to Explain** Explain why a square is always symmetric.

_____

_____

_____

# Problem Solving:
# Make and Test Generalizations

When you make a generalization, you make a broad statement about something that a group has in common. A generalization helps you find patterns. When you make a generalization, it is important to test it to be sure it is correct.

**Example:** 1 × 24 = 24   1 × 93 = 93
          1 × 126 = 126

**Generalization:** A number multiplied by 1 is itself.

**Test:** If I multiply a different number by 1, it is also equal to itself. For example, 1 × 2 = 2; 1 × 3 = 3; 1 × 4 = 4, etc.; any number multiplied by 1 is itself. My generalization is correct.

In some cases, it is possible to find more than one correct generalization:

**Example:** Jessica found a red pencil, 3 red pens, and 2 red markers in her backpack.

**Generalization #1:** The things Jessica found are all writing instruments.

**Generalization #2:** The things Jessica found are all red.

**Test:** I can write with a pencil, a pen, and a marker. Also, the pencil, the pens, and the markers are all red. My generalizations are correct.

---

1. Randy has 2 tennis balls, 6 marbles, and 1 orange in his desk drawer. What generalization can you make about these things?

   _____

2. This week, Sandy was out sick on Monday and Tuesday. Last week, Jared was out sick on Thursday and Friday. The week before, Elisa was out sick on Wednesday and Thursday. What generalization can you make about these three students' absences? Can you make a second generalization?

   _____

   _____

3. Write down the first three multiples of 15, 20, and 25. What generalization can you make about all multiples of 5?

   _____

   _____

# Problem Solving:
# Make and Test Generalizations

For Exercises **1** through **3**, use the images to make a
generalization and test your answer.

1.

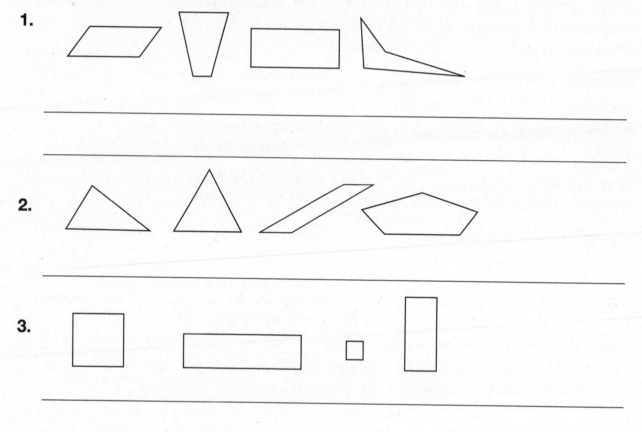

2.

3.

4. Which statement below is a good generalization about
   all polygons?

   **A** All polygons have right angles.

   **B** All polygons are closed figures.

   **C** All polygons have parallel sides.

   **D** All polygons are quadrilaterals.

5. **Writing to Explain** Try to draw a triangle with 2 right or
   obtuse angles. What generalizations can you make about
   the angles of a triangle? Explain.

   _____

   _____

# The Distributive Property

You can use the Distributive Property to multiply mentally.

**Example A.** Evaluate $7 \times 53$.

$7 \times 53$

Break 53 apart into $50 + 3$.

$7 \times (50 + 3)$

Then distribute the 7 to each part.

$(7 \times 50) + (7 \times 3)$

Multiply.

$350 + 21$

Add the products.

$371$

**Example B.** Evaluate $5(42) - 5(2)$. Remember $5(42)$ means $5 \times 42$.

Use the Distributive Property in reverse.

$5(42) - 5(2)$

Join 42 and 2 using the minus sign.

$5 (42 - 2)$

Subtract.

$5 \times 40$

Multiply the difference by 5.

$200$

Find each missing number.

**1.** $8 \times (30 + 2) = (8 \times \underline{\hspace{1cm}}) + (8 \times 2)$ **2.** $(6 \times \underline{\hspace{1cm}}) - (6 \times 7) = 6 \times (37 - 7)$

**3.** $8(28) = 8(20) + 8(\underline{\hspace{1cm}})$ **4.** $3(22) + 3(4) = 3(\underline{\hspace{1cm}}) + 3(6)$

Use the Distributive Property and mental math to evaluate.

**5.** $6(24)$ _____ **6.** $4(13) - 4(3)$ _____

**7.** $7(24 + 6)$ _____ **8.** $2(72)$ _____

**9.** $9(12) + 9(3)$_____ **10.** $5(24 - 3)$ _____

**11. Number Sense** What are two other ways to write $9(46)$?

_____

Name _____

# The Distributive Property

Find each missing number.

**1.** $8 \times (30 + 2) = (8 \times$ _____$) + (8 \times 2)$

**2.** $8(94) = 8($_____$) + 8(4)$

**3.** $5(45 + 5) = 5($_____$)$

**4.** $9(42) - 9(4) = 9(30) + 9($_____$)$

Use the Distributive Property and mental math to evaluate.

**5.** $3(58 - 8)$ _____

**6.** $7(31 + 19)$ _____

**7.** $9(72)$ _____

**8.** $4(26) - 4(16)$ _____

**9.** $8(41) + 8(5)$ _____

**10.** $5(22 - 5)$ _____

**11.** Describe the mental math steps you would use to find $7(42)$.

_____

_____

**12. Number Sense** Use mental math to evaluate the expression $6(31) + 6(4) - 6(15)$.

_____

**13. Geometry** Write an expression for the area of this rectangle. Evaluate your expression to find the area.

20 cm    4 cm

8 cm

_____

**14. Algebra** Which expression is equal to $12m + 12n$?

   **A** $12mn$

   **B** $12m + n$

   **C** $12m - 12n$

   **D** $12(m + n)$

Name _____

# Using Variables to Write Expressions

A variable represents a quantity that can change. To use a variable to write an algebraic expression, you need to decide which operation is appropriate. To help you, some words and phrases are listed below.

| Word phrase | Variable | Operation | Algebraic Expression |
|---|---|---|---|
| ten **more than** a number $b$ | $b$ | Addition | $b + 10$ |
| the **sum** of 8 and a number $c$ | $c$ | | $8 + c$ |
| five **less than** a number $d$ | $d$ | Subtraction | $d - 5$ |
| 15 **decreased by** a number $e$ | $e$ | | $15 - e$ |
| the **product** of 8 and a number $f$ | $f$ | Multiplication | $8f$ |
| 19 **times** a number $g$ | $g$ | | $19g$ |
| the quotient of a number $h$ **divided by** 2 | $h$ | Division | $h \div 2$ |
| a number $i$ **divided into** 50 | $i$ | | $50 \div i$ |

Write each algebraic expression.

1. a number $m$ **divided by** 6 _____

2. the **sum** of 4 and a number $n$ _____     3. 4 **times** a number $p$ _____

4. a number $n$ **divided into** 7 _____     5. 3 **less than** a number $r$ _____

6. *a* fewer grapes than 12 _____     7. $q$ sandwiches at $8 each _____

8. Each fourth grader has 5 notebooks. Write an algebraic expression to represent the number of notebooks the entire class has.

   Identify the operation. _____     Write the expression. _____

9. **Writing to Explain** Write an algebraic expression to represent the situation below. Explain how the expression relates to the situation.

   Some monkeys share 7 bananas equally among themselves.

   _____

   _____

Name _____

# Using Variables to Write Expressions

Write each algebraic expression.

1. 4 more than a number $b$ _____

2. twice a number $a$ _____

3. 20 less than a number $c$ _____

4. the product of 5 and a number $d$ _____

5. 30 divided by a number $f$ _____

6. the sum of a number $e$ and 3 _____

7. 9 more stripes than a number $h$ _____

8. 14 fewer hats than five times a number $i$ _____

9. Chad has $80. He buys a book. Which expression shows how much money Chad has left?

   **A** $s + 80$

   **B** $80 - s$

   **C** $80s$

   **D** $s \div 80$

10. A coffee shop has booths and counter seating. Each booth can seat 4 people. Another 20 people can sit at the counter. Which expression shows how many customers can be seated in the coffee shop?

    **A** $20b - 4$      **B** $20b + 4$      **C** $4b - 20$      **D** $4b + 20$

11. Sofia bought some flats of daisies. Each flat holds 9 daisies. Sofia has planted 10 daisies. Is $9x + 10$ a reasonable way to represent the number of daisies that Sofia has left to plant? Explain your answer.

    _____

    _____

    _____

Name _____

# Using Patterns to Divide

You can use basic facts and patterns to divide mentally.

| **Using basic facts** | **Using patterns** |
|---|---|
| What is 140 ÷ 70? | What is 4,200 ÷ 70? |
| Think: **140 ÷ 70** is the same as **14** tens ÷ 7 tens. | 4,200 ÷ 70 is the same as 420 ÷ 7. |
| 14 ÷ 7 = 2 | Think: 42 ÷ 7 = 6, so 420 ÷ 7 = 60. |
| So, 140 ÷ 70 = 2. | So, 4,200 ÷ 70 = 60. |

Find each quotient. Use mental math.

**1.** 210 ÷ 70 = _____

**2.** 360 ÷ 30 = _____

**3.** 400 ÷ 80 = _____

**4.** 1,200 ÷ 60 = _____

**5.** 4,000 ÷ 40 = _____

**6.** 4,800 ÷ 80 = _____

**7.** 2,700 ÷ 30 = _____

**8.** 3,500 ÷ 50 = _____

**9. Number Sense** How is dividing 140 by 20 the same as dividing 1,400 by 200?

_____

_____

_____

**10. Writing to Explain** Explain how you can use mental math to determine that 28,000 ÷ 70 = 400.

_____

_____

_____

# Using Patterns to Divide

In **1** through **4**, find each quotient. Use mental math.

**1.** $160 \div 40 = 16$ tens $\div 4$ tens = _____

**2.** $6{,}300 \div 70 = 630$ tens $\div 7$ tens = _____

**3.** $140 \div 70 = 14$ tens $\div 7$ tens = _____

**4.** $3{,}700 \div 10 = 370$ tens $\div 1$ ten = _____

Use mental math to answer the following questions.

**5.** If the cans are divided evenly among the shelves, how many cans are on each shelf?

_____

**6.** If the cans are divided evenly among the rows on each shelf, how many cans are in each row?

_____

| Supermarket Storage | |
| --- | --- |
| Cans for sale | 1,200 |
| Shelves of cans | 10 |
| Rows per shelf | 6 |

**7. Estimation** Suppose there are 387 balls in the gym. If each bin can hold 48 balls, estimate the number of bins that will be needed to hold all the balls.

_____

_____

**8. Algebra** If $300{,}000 \div h = 6$, what is the value of $h$?

**A** 50      **B** 500      **C** 5,000      **D** 50,000

**9.** Solve the equation $n \times 50 = 5{,}000$. Explain your solution.

_____

_____

Name _____

# Connecting Decimal and Whole Number Numeration

Whole number place values and decimal place values are shown below. Each place value to the left is ten times as much as the place value to its right.

| Thousands | Hundreds | Tens | Ones | Decimal | Tenths | Hundredths | Thousandths |
|-----------|----------|------|------|---------|--------|------------|-------------|
| 1,000 | 100 | 10 | 1 | . | $0.1 = \frac{1}{10}$ | $0.01 = \frac{1}{100}$ | $0.001 = \frac{1}{1,000}$ |

For example, 1 ten is equal to 10 ones.      In 1 tenth, there are 10 hundredths.

Write the place value for the underlined digit. Then write the total value of the underlined digit.

**1.** 348.6̲05

place value: _____

total value: _____

**2.** 2̲,348.56

place value: _____

total value: _____

**3.** 449.65̲4

place value: _____

total value: _____

**4.** 3̲48.56

place value: _____

total value: _____

**5. Number Sense** Does 6 have a greater value in 13.6 or in 83.06? Explain.

_____

_____

**6. Writing to Explain** Cassie ran one lap around the indoor track in 32.09 seconds. She ran a second lap in 32.1 seconds. Did it take more or less time for Cassie to run the second lap? Explain.

_____

Name _____

# Connecting Decimal and Whole Number Numeration

Write the place value for the underlined digit.

1. 5,009.94<u>1</u>

_____

2. 456.<u>9</u>6

_____

3. 3,116.<u>8</u>52

_____

4. 2,440.50<u>4</u>

_____

5. 599.0<u>4</u>

_____

6. 387.5<u>6</u>9

_____

7. <u>6</u>98.07

_____

8. <u>4</u>,456.87

_____

9. 9<u>8</u>6.54

_____

10. Which decimal has the same digit in the hundredths place and the hundreds place?

  A 145.54      C 965.439

  B 783.38      D 5,486.649

11. Donna bought 4.356 pounds of cheese. What is the value of each of the digits in 4.356?

_____

_____

_____

_____

12. Which is equal to 30 hundredths?

  A 3 thousandths   C 3 tens

  B 3 tenths        D 3 thousands

13. Bill's average speed in the bicycle race was 29.215 miles per hour. What is the place value of the 1 in that number?

_____

14. Kathy has 2 tenths of a dollar. Tom has 10 hundredths of a dollar. Is Kathy's amount or is Tom's amount more?

_____

_____

Name _____

# Rounding Decimals

You can use the number line below to help you round 7.14 to the nearest whole number. Is 7.14 closer to 7 or 8?

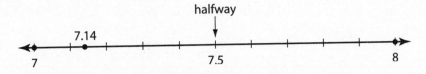

7.14 is less than halfway to 8. So, 7.14 is closer to 7.

A number line can help you round 8.762 to the nearest tenth. Is 8.762 closer to 8.7 or 8.8?

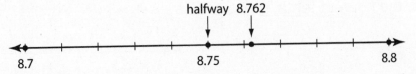

8.762 is more than halfway to 8.8. So, 8.762 is closer to 8.8.

Round each number to the place of the underlined digit.

**1.** 0.<u>7</u>234

_____

**2.** <u>4</u>.526

_____

**3.** 3.86<u>2</u>9

_____

**4.** 25.<u>1</u>47

_____

For **5** and **6**, use the table at the right.

**5.** Round the number of inches of precipitation in Tallahassee to the nearest tenth.

_____

| Inches of Precipitation in 2007 | |
|---|---|
| Daytona | 45.02 |
| Tallahassee | 44.47 |
| Orlando | 38.49 |

**6.** Round the number of inches of precipitation in Orlando to the nearest whole number.

_____

**7. Number Sense** Marc earned $8.76 per hour working at the library. Round his wage to the nearest ten cents.

_____

Name _____

# Rounding Decimals

Round each number to the place of the underlined digit.

1. 17.<u>2</u>3    _____

2. 569.<u>9</u>1    _____

3. 2.17<u>8</u>5    _____

4. 26.<u>0</u>62    _____

5. **Reasoning** Name two different numbers that round to 9.2 when rounded to the nearest tenth.

_____

_____

In early 2007, a U.S. dollar was equivalent to about 0.51 British pounds and about 1.17 Canadian dollars. Round each country's U.S. dollar equivalent to the nearest tenth of a dollar.

6. Britain    _____

7. Canada    _____

In 2007, the price of wheat was $10.03 per bushel. The price of soybeans was $11.93 per bushel. Round the price per bushel of wheat and soybeans to the nearest whole dollar.

8. wheat    _____

9. soybeans    _____

10. **Number Sense** Which number rounds to 600 when rounded to the nearest whole number?

    **A** 600.83    **B** 599.1    **C** 600.5    **D** 599.72

11. Write a definition of rounding in your own words.

_____

_____

Name _____

# Estimating Quotients with 2-Digit Divisors

You can use compatible numbers to estimate a quotient.

Estimate 228 ÷ 19.

**Step 1:** Find compatible numbers for 228 and 19.

Think: 20 can be divided evenly by 2.

200 is close to 228 and 20 is close to 19.

200 and 20 are compatible numbers.

**Step 2:** Divide. Use patterns to help you, if possible.

Think: 200 ÷ 20 is the same as
    20 tens ÷ 2 tens.

20 ÷ 2 = 10
So, 200 ÷ 20 = 10.

Estimate each quotient using compatible numbers.

1. 540 ÷ 91 _____

2. 2,777 ÷ 74 _____

3. 29,952 ÷ 98 _____

4. 288 ÷ 37 _____

5. 1,784 ÷ 32 _____

6. 6,127 ÷ 32 _____

At Cambridge Elementary School, fourth-grade students are saving money for a summer trip to a theme park.

7. The amount Aubrey has saved is about how many times as great as the amount Joe has saved?

| Student | Amount Saved |
|---------|--------------|
| Rebecca | $110 |
| Joe | $ 92 |
| Ken | $225 |
| Atiyah | $ 53 |
| Aubrey | $189 |

_____

_____

# Estimating Quotients with 2-Digit Divisors

In **1** through **4**, estimate the quotients using compatible numbers.

**1.** $198 \div 41 =$ _____

**2.** $202 \div 52 =$ _____

**3.** $1,745 \div 63 =$ _____

**4.** $7,810 \div 22 =$ _____

**5. Reasoning** How do you know that 8,100 and 90 are NOT the best compatible numbers to use when estimating the quotient of $9,269 \div 88$?

_____

_____

_____

**6.** Suppose there are 18 children at Georgi's party. Georgi's dad has 59 balloons and hands them out to the children. Estimate the number of balloons each child will receive.

_____

**7.** At a department store, a package of 8 t-shirts costs $38. Estimate how much each t-shirt costs.

_____

**8. Number Sense** Which is the closest estimate for $1,219 \div 44$?

**A** 3          **B** 13          **C** 30          **D** 300

**9.** Explain how to estimate $425 \div 8$.

_____

_____

_____

# Modeling Addition and Subtraction of Decimals

## Adding decimals using a hundredths grid:

Add 0.26 + 0.12.

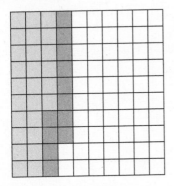

**Step 1:** Shade 26 squares to show 0.26.

**Step 2:** Use a different color. Shade 12 squares to show 0.12.

**Step 3:** Count all the squares that are shaded. How many hundredths are shaded in all? Write the decimal for the total shaded squares: 0.38.

So, 0.26 + 0.12 = 0.38.

## Subtracting decimals using a hundredths grid:

Subtract 0.52 − 0.33.

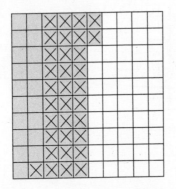

**Step 1:** Shade 52 squares to show 0.52.

**Step 2:** Cross out 33 squares to show 0.33.

**Step 3:** Count the squares that are shaded but not crossed out. Write the decimal: 0.19.

So, 0.52 − 0.33 = 0.19.

---

Add or subtract. You may use hundredths grids to help.

**1.** 0.42 + 0.37 = _____

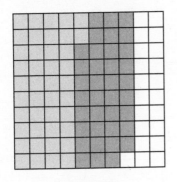

**2.** 0.37 − 0.31 = _____

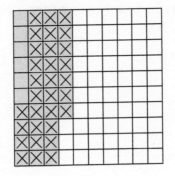

Name _____

# Modeling Addition and Subtraction of Decimals

Add or subtract. Use hundredths grids if necessary.

**1.** 0.24 + 0.53 = _____

**2.** 0.24 − 0.18 = _____

**3.** 0.88 + 0.25 = _____

**4.** 2.36 + 0.85 = _____

**5.** 0.61 − 0.47 = _____

**6.** 1.20 − 0.53 = _____

**7.** 2.20 − 1.97 = _____

**8.** 0.52 + 0.89 = _____

**9. Number Sense** Is the difference of
2.45 − 1.54 less than or greater than 1?

_____

**10.** A jar of oregano holds 0.9 ounce. A jar of cayenne pepper
holds 0.75 ounce. How much more does a jar of oregano
hold?

_____

**11.** Add: 1.75 + 1.29

**A** 2.04          **B** 2.94          **C** 3.04          **D** 3.14

**12.** Explain how to use hundredths grids to
find 1.86 − 0.75.

_____

_____

_____

# Relating Division to Multiplication of Fractions

How can you divide by a fraction?

Dividing a whole number by a fraction

| $2 \div \dfrac{1}{3}$ | Think: How can I divide two into one-thirds? |
|---|---|
| **1.** Two is the sum of one plus one. | $2 \quad = \quad 1 \quad + \quad 1$ |
| **2.** Each one is the sum of three one-thirds. | $\dfrac{1}{3} + \dfrac{1}{3} + \dfrac{1}{3} \quad + \quad \dfrac{1}{3} + \dfrac{1}{3} + \dfrac{1}{3}$ |
| **3.** Count the number of one-thirds. | **6** |
| **Check** To divide a whole number by a fraction, multiply the whole number by the reciprocal of the fraction. | $2 \div \dfrac{1}{3} = 2 \times \dfrac{3}{1} = \dfrac{2}{1} \times \dfrac{3}{1} = \dfrac{6}{1} = 6$ |

| $3 \div \dfrac{3}{4}$ | Think: How can I divide three into three-fourths? |
|---|---|
| **1.** Three is the sum of one plus one plus one. | $3 = \quad 1 \quad + \quad 1 \quad + \quad 1$ |
| **2.** Each one is the sum of one three-fourths and one one-fourth. | $\dfrac{3}{4} + \dfrac{1}{4} \quad + \quad \dfrac{3}{4} + \dfrac{1}{4} \quad + \quad \dfrac{3}{4} + \dfrac{1}{4}$ |
| | $\dfrac{3}{4} + \dfrac{3}{4} + \dfrac{3}{4} \quad + \quad \dfrac{1}{4} + \dfrac{1}{4} + \dfrac{1}{4}$ |
| **3.** Count the number of three-fourths. | $\dfrac{3}{4} + \dfrac{3}{4} + \dfrac{3}{4} \quad + \qquad \dfrac{3}{4}$ |
| **Check** Multiply the whole number by the reciprocal of the fraction. | **4** |
| | $3 \div \dfrac{3}{4} = 3 \times \dfrac{4}{3} = \dfrac{3}{1} \times \dfrac{4}{3} = \dfrac{12}{3} = 4$ |

Draw a picture that shows each division and write the answer.

**1.** $2 \div \dfrac{1}{2}$ _____

**2.** $2 \div \dfrac{2}{3}$ _____

Name _____

# Relating Division to Multiplication of Fractions

In **1** and **2**, use the picture to find each quotient.

**1.** How many thirds are in 1?

_____

**2.** How many thirds are in 7?

_____

In **3** and **4**, draw a picture to find each quotient.

**3.** $3 \div \frac{1}{2}$

**4.** $4 \div \frac{1}{8}$

_____

_____

In **5** and **6**, use multiplication to find each quotient.

**5.** $6 \div \frac{1}{3}$

**6.** $5 \div \frac{1}{10}$

_____

_____

**7.** Julie bought 3 yards of cloth to make holiday napkin rings. If she needs $\frac{3}{4}$ of a yard to make each ring, how many rings can she make?

_____

**8.** When you divide a whole number by a fraction with a numerator of 1, explain how you can find the quotient.

_____

_____

_____

# Multiplying Fractions and Whole Numbers

You can find the product of a fraction and a whole number.

Francesco needs $\frac{2}{3}$ yard of fabric to sew a shirt. How many yards of fabric will Francesco need to sew 6 shirts?

**Step 1:** Multiply the numerator by the whole number.

$2 \times 6 = 12$

**Step 2:** Place the product over the denominator. Simplify if possible.

$\frac{12}{3} = 4$ yards of fabric

Remember: In word problems, "of" often means "multiply."

Example: $\frac{3}{5}$ of $15 = \frac{3}{5} \times 15$

In **1** through **4**, find each product. Simplify if possible.

1. $\frac{2}{3} \times 30 =$ _____

2. $\frac{3}{4}$ of $28 =$ _____

3. $\frac{7}{8} \times 32 =$ _____

4. $\frac{3}{7}$ of $35 =$ _____

For Exercises **5** through **7**, use the table to the right.

5. What is $\frac{2}{7}$ the speed of a cheetah? _____

6. What is $\frac{1}{5}$ the speed of a lion? _____

7. What is $\frac{1}{5}$ the speed of a rabbit? _____

| Animal | Speed (in mi/h) |
|--------|-----------------|
| Lion | 50 |
| Cheetah | 70 |
| Rabbit | 35 |

Name _____

# Multiplying Fractions and Whole Numbers

Find each product.

1. $\frac{1}{2}$ of 96 = _____

2. $\frac{3}{7}$ of 28 = _____

3. $\frac{3}{4} \times 36 =$ _____

4. $45 \times \frac{4}{9} =$ _____

5. $56 \times \frac{7}{8} =$ _____

6. $42 \times \frac{3}{7} =$ _____

7. $\frac{1}{2}$ of 76 = _____

8. $\frac{3}{8}$ of 56 = _____

9. $\frac{1}{10} \times 200 =$ _____

10. $84 \times \frac{1}{4} =$ _____

11. $64 \times \frac{5}{8}$ _____

12. $20 \times \frac{11}{20} =$ _____

13. $\frac{3}{8}$ of 48 = _____

14. $\frac{1}{6}$ of 66 = _____

15. $\frac{4}{5} \times 30 =$ _____

16. $42 \times \frac{3}{6} =$ _____

17. $72 \times \frac{5}{8} =$ _____

18. $18 \times \frac{1}{3} =$ _____

19. $\frac{5}{6} \times 66 =$ _____

20. $\frac{11}{12} \times 72 =$ _____

21. $\frac{6}{7} \times 35 =$ _____

22. Complete the table by writing the product of each expression in the box below it. Use a pattern to find each product. Explain the pattern.

| $\frac{1}{2} \times 64$ | $\frac{1}{4} \times 64$ | $\frac{1}{8} \times 64$ | $\frac{1}{16} \times 64$ |
|---|---|---|---|
|  |  |  |  |

_____

23. **Reasoning** If $\frac{1}{3}$ of 1 is $\frac{1}{3}$, what is $\frac{1}{3}$ of 2, 3, and 4? _____

24. Which is $\frac{1}{3}$ of 225?

   **A** 75          **B** 113          **C** 150          **D** 450

25. Explain why $\frac{1}{4}$ of 4 equals one whole.

_____

_____